PULSE

PUMPING LIFE INTO YOUR KIDS MINISTRY

KIDZMATTER

EDITED BY **RYAN AND BETH FRANK**
WITH **ROGER FIELDS, JIM WIDEMAN, LARRY FOWLER, TINA HOUSER & MORE**

Pulse: Pumping Life Into Your Kids Ministry

edited by Ryan and Beth Frank
copyright ©2014 KidzMatter Inc.

Trade paperback ISBN: 9781938624759
Ebook ISBN: 9781938624766

Cover design by Mike DeLeon

Pulse is also available on Amazon Kindle, Barnes & Noble Nook and Apple iBooks.

For more information, visit KidzMatter.com and follow us at:

 /KidzMatter

 /KidzMatterInc

 /KidzMatter

 /KidzMatter

CONTENTS

INTRODUCTION: WHAT MATTERS MOST
RYAN & BETH FRANK 7

I. LEADERSHIP MATTERS IN CHILDREN'S MINISTRY
GREG BAIRD 15

2. THE EVOLUTION TO FAMILY MINISTRY
TREVOR LEE 23

3. KEEPING LIFE SIMPLE
JIM WIDEMAN 33

4. WHY KIDS (REALLY) MISBEHAVE
DR. RICK CHROMEY 41

5. RECRUITING FROM A 3-LEGGED STOOL
LARRY FOWLER 47

6. THE 10 ESSENTIAL FACTORS IN VOLUNTEER RETENTION
JOSH DENHART 53

7. CHILDREN'S CHURCH ESSENTIALS
DICK GRUBER 61

8. MAKE IT REAL
KEITH FERRIN 69

9. LEADING THROUGH CHANGE
MICHAEL BAYNE 75

10. PLAY THE BALL WHERE THE MONKEY DROPS IT
ROGER FIELDS 81

II. THE BIG BOX OF POTENTIAL
MIKE JOHNSON 89

12. NO COOKIE-CUTTER CHILDREN'S MINISTRIES
LYNDA FREEMAN 95

13. DISCIPLING CHILDREN
TAMERA KRAFT 101

14. WHO'S YOUR PAUL?
JENNY FUNDERBURKE 107

15. BI-VOCATIONAL CHILDREN'S MINISTRY
LINDSEY WHITNEY 113

16. SOLUTIONS FOR SMALLER CHURCHES
DIENNA GOSCHA 121

17. HOW TO TALK TO KIDS ABOUT THE HARD STUFF
BETH GUCKENBERGER 127

18. LET THE CHILDREN COME TO ME
KATIE WETHERBEE...135

19. I WANT TO BE KNOWN
TINA HOUSER..139

20. HOW DIVORCE IMPACTS A CHILD'S RELATIONSHIP WITH GOD
LINDA RANSON JACOBS 145

21. ENCOUNTERING THE BIBLICAL NARRATIVE
JEREMY MAVIS 153

22. STANDING ON THE SHOULDERS OF GIANTS
CRAIG JOHNSON...161

23. HELPING EVERY PARENT TAKE A NEXT STEP
JONATHAN CLIFF 169

24. THE PROCRASTINATION TRAP
BRIAN DOLLAR 175

25. MARGIN = MINISTRY
MATT NORMAN 181

26. TRAINING TEENAGERS TO BE CHILDREN'S MINISTRY LEADERS
STEVEN KNIGHT 189

27. HEART VERSUS HEAD
GLORIA LEE..197

28. IT'S ABOUT THEM, NOT YOU
MELISSA MACDONALD..203

29. I WANNA BE LIKE YOU
TINA HOUSER...109

30. SUCCESSION: WHO'S NEXT?
RICARDO MILLER 215

31. LEADING VOLUNTEERS
GLORIA LEE..223

32. 5 STEPS AND 1 BIG IDEA TO HELP PARENTS BECOME ALLIES
NAOMI CRAMER OVERTON...229

33. WHY KIDS WORSHIP IS WORTH IT
BOB SINGLETON..235

34. JANE AUSTEN'S TAKE ON CURRICULUM
LINDA WEDDLE...243

35. HONEY I SHRUNK THE GOSPEL
SAM LUCE..249

36. THE SQUIRREL SYNDROME
RON BROOKS..255

37. THE PURITY AND POWER OF WORSHIP
YANCY...261

38. PRAY ABOUT IT
KEITH FERRIN...269

WHAT MATTERS MOST

BY RYAN & BETH FRANK

I love to meet people who have rolled up their sleeves and are faithfully working in children's ministry. As I travel across the country, I meet some of the most creative, passionate people on the planet. But there's one thing that bugs me when I talk to them. I'll tell you what it is in just a minute.

I meet people with gray hair who have been Sunday school teachers for fifty years. I meet college kids with cool t-shirts and ripped jeans who are in their first year. I meet stay-at-home moms who teach kids' church every other month. They're all great people, but something about them bugs me. I'll tell you in just a minute.

Some people are big into small groups. Others prefer to have 100 kids in a room for an hour. Some people dig Popsicle sticks and hot glue. Others avoid crafts like a plague. To some "multimedia" means laminated flash cards. To others it's three flat screens on the wall with killer sound and lights.

7

As great as these people are, some of them bug me. I'll tell you why in just a minute.

I meet people in children's ministry who like video-driven curriculum. Then I meet someone who thinks virtue-based is the way to go. The next guy I see tells me why he's all about being game-based. They are all great people, but something bugs me. I'll tell you what it is ... right now!

The thing that bugs me about children's ministry leaders I meet is that one out of four will always ask me this question: "How big is your church?"

I've asked myself why people would bother asking this question.

Theory 1: They are genuinely interested in knowing about my church in the small town of Sweetser, Indiana, and what my church is like. This is the benefit-of-the-doubt theory.

Theory 2: They don't care a thing about my church in Sweetser, Indiana. They just want to know how many people go to my church because they equate success with size. This is the big-equals-success theory. I can't read minds, but I think 90% of them ask about the size of my church for this very reason.

Here's what a lot of people think: A church of 20,000 must be more successful than a church of 5,000. A church of 5,000 must be more successful than a church of 200. And so on. Really?

What defines success in the church? What about in children's ministry? Is it big numbers? A children's ministry building that looks like Disney World? A high-tech check-in system with bar code scanners? There's nothing wrong with those things, but they don't measure success—at least not according to Paul.

In the New Testament, Pastor Paul has a lot to say about ministry. Nothing made him redline like the work of the church and lives being changed through Jesus Christ. It fired him up! Let's look at his letter to the church in Rome.

First, I thank my God through Jesus Christ for all of you, because your faith is being reported all over the world. God, whom I serve with my whole heart in preaching the gospel of his Son, is my witness how constantly I remember you in my prayers at all times; and I pray that now at last by God's will the way may be opened for me to come to you. I long to see you so that I may impart to you some spiritual gift to make you strong—that is, that you and I may be mutually encouraged by each other's faith. I do not want you to be unaware, brothers, that I planned many times to come to you (but have been prevented from doing so until now) in order that I might have a harvest among you, just as I have had among the other Gentiles. I am obligated both to Greeks and non-Greeks, both to the wise and the foolish. That is why I am so eager to preach the gospel also to you who are at Rome. I am not ashamed of the gospel . . . (Romans 1:8–16, NIV).

Let's use this passage of scripture to guide our thoughts on the topic of what really matters in children's ministry.

PAUL GOT THE POINT.

When is the last time you paused to thank God for the privilege of serving children and their families? As you read the passage above, you see that Paul wasn't scrambling to discover what he was suppose to be doing. He got it. This means we need to listen to what he has to say.

The point in five words: Lives changed by God's Word.

"Your faith is being reported all over the world." (Romans 1:8, NIV)

Wherever Paul went, people were talking about what God was doing at the church in Rome. This was before Facebook and Instagram. Paul wasn't following the Romans on Twitter or getting text messages from the deacons in Rome. People were being changed and the word was spreading like wild-fire. The million-dollar question in children's ministry leadership is not about a program, model or leadership style. It's this: Are kids being changed to become like Christ? And this is where I believe you find the point of children's ministry.

Kids being changed to become like Christ.

Stop reading for just a moment and get a fresh reminder that God is at work. You are still reading! Seriously, stop and think about it. God wants to work today just as He did in Paul's day. He wants to show up (big time) in your ministry.

How does God work? How are lives changed to become like Christ? The primary method is found in the next verse. He chooses to work "in preaching the gospel of His Son." (Romans 1:9, NIV). Never replace the centrality of God's Word in children's ministry. It's in the context of God's Word that lives are changed.

Discover the point, and then get serious about prayer.

"How constantly I remember you in my prayers at all times."
(Romans 1:9–10, NIV)

Your best intentions in children's ministry are not good enough. You'll accomplish very little without God's help. I'm not talking about tangibles, like a record-setting VBS or a new facility, but those eternally important intangibles such as lives being changed to become like Christ. What power do you have to ensure that the enemy stays away and that the children in your church will long to walk with God? You don't have any power, but God does!

There's a volunteer on our children's ministry team who understands the power of prayer. Recently, while praying with him, my heart was warmed and tears swelled in my eyes as he prayed for at least one hundred kids by name. This man knows how to pray, and it got my attention. (I believe it got someone else's attention too!)

Identify the point, and then cover it with love.

"I long to see you so that I may impart to you some spiritual gift to make you strong." (Romans 1:11, NIV)

One mark of great leaders is a growing capacity to love people. Can you pick up on the love in Paul's words? Look at this passage from another translation: "The longer this waiting goes on, the deeper the ache. I so want to be there to deliver God's gift in person and watch you grow stronger right before my eyes!" (Romans 1:11, *The Message*)

Identify the point, and then never give up.

"I am obligated." (Romans 1:14, NIV)

Paul went on to communicate the commitment he had to the ministry. Paul wasn't in ministry for personal reasons or because someone asked him to fill a slot. He served because of a sense of obligation. I challenge you to tell God that you're a "lifer" in children's ministry until He lets you know otherwise.

There are times when children's ministry is rewarding. It's great when a child says that she can't wait to come back next Sunday or a child tells you that he wants to ask Jesus to be his Savior.

However, there are other times when the ministry isn't as rewarding and the kids aren't as receptive. (You all know what I'm talking about.) On those days, continue to do your best because you're under obligation to God and to those kids and families whom you're serving. Don't quit! Say it with me: "I am not going to quit!" (Seriously, say it out loud right now!) May God give you the grace to say these words and mean them!

The point (changed lives) centers on the Gospel.

"I am not ashamed of the gospel." (Romans 1:16, NIV)

Methodology and programs change, but God's measurement of success never changes. Sometimes we look for creative, innovative, dynamic, exciting ways to succeed while overlooking the obvious. Want to know what's really important to God? Lives changed with the Gospel!

If the Gospel is so important, we need to make sure we understand what it is. Let's go to Jesus and hear what He has to say. "The thief comes only to steal and kill and destroy. I came that they may have life and have it abundantly." (John 10:10, ESV) The Gospel is the message of Christ (His death, burial and resurrection) and the abundant life that He offers.

Success is not found in programs. There's nothing wrong with sporting events, family services and concerts, but good programs don't bring success.

Success is not found in environments. You don't have to cough up thousands of dollars to make your building look like a theme park to be successful. There's nothing wrong with themed environments, but there are more important things than paint and plasma screens.

Success is not found in the latest and greatest stuff. Success doesn't automatically equal having a high-ticket check-in system or a brand new playground.

Success is not found in the size of a ministry. We'll never reach a generation by pointing to the size of our church or being proud about what we've done.

Programs. Environments. Stuff. Size. These are all good, but they don't indicate success.

Success in God's eyes is found in being faithful to what He has called you to do. Faithfully proclaiming the Gospel week after week—that's success. Lives changed to become like Christ—that's success.

 Ryan Frank serves as the CEO of KidzMatter and Vice President of Innovative Strategies at Awana. Ryan and his wife, Beth, are also the publishers of *K! Magazine*. Ryan served as a children's pastor for 15 years at the church where he came to the Lord at age five.

CHAPTER 1

LEADERSHIP MATTERS IN CHILDREN'S MINISTRY

BY **GREG BAIRD**

The "dream job" I had landed wasn't working out so well. Being John Maxwell's Children's Pastor wasn't supposed to be so hard. Yet here I was, lacking volunteers, constantly putting out fires and spending way too many hours trying to make it all happen.

I talked to other children's pastors and some were dealing with the same issues I was dealing with, but some were not. What was the difference?

An interview with an intern helped me discover the problem. She knocked on my office door and asked if she could interview me about children's ministry. She began asking about each area of ministry—Sunday school, kids' church, the nursery, Awana, midweek programs, etc. As she asked about the leadership structure of each area, the answer was always the same: "I was in charge." The full responsibility of every single area in my children's ministry fell to me. I had not developed leaders in my ministry, and, in fact, had been so good at keeping the responsibilities for myself, that few leaders were even offering to step up and help anymore.

Suddenly the words that John Maxwell had been saying to us over and over again had new meaning. His mantra was "Everything rises and falls on leadership." I could glibly repeat that to anyone who would listen, but suddenly I understood its meaning to me: *leadership really does matter in children's ministry!*

IF ... THEN ... SO ...

I realized through that interview with the intern that, *if* everything rises and falls on leadership, *then* my ministry will only rise to the level that I and my leaders can take it, *so* increasing the leadership capacity in my ministry must be a very high priority.

It wasn't. And instead of rising, my ministry was falling—fast! Instead of running around trying to do everything myself, I needed to invest in developing leaders to lead with me. But I had no idea how to do that.

MAKING LEADERSHIP MATTER IN YOUR MINISTRY

Understand the definition of leadership.

Before we can truly lead or begin to develop leaders in our ministry, we have to understand what leadership really is. For our purposes, we'll use this definition: *leadership is the ability to influence others toward the pursuit of a worthy vision.*

Those who influence, lead. Leaders don't poke, prod and manipulate. They clearly articulate that worthy vision, define the route to pursuing it, lead by example and develop others to lead with them.

Lead yourself in order to lead others.

Leading others begins by leading yourself. If you don't lead yourself well, you won't lead others for long. Often, though, in our eagerness to lead others well, we forget to lead ourselves.

First, leading yourself means doing the things necessary to continue to grow and thrive in all aspects of life. Luke 2:52 provides a great example of what areas to focus on from the life of Jesus. It says that Jesus grew "in wisdom and in stature, and in favor with God and with all the people." Intellectually, physically, spiritually and relationally, Jesus was growing. The disciplines we must practice in each of these areas will be different for different leaders, but some general questions to consider might be:

- What is my specific plan to continue learning in the areas I need to learn in?

- Am I honoring God in the way I am caring for my body?

- Am I practicing spiritual disciplines and making sure my relationship with God is healthy and not being replaced by my service in the church?

- Knowing that life, ministry and leadership always happens best in the context of relationships, am I being careful to intentionally develop relationships with others?

Second, leading yourself means protecting your heart. Proverbs 4:23 says, "Above all else, guard your heart, for it affects everything you do." Character issues can undermine your leadership and slowly erode it until you have no influence. Major character lapses can completely destroy your ability to influence. Make sure you have guard rails to protect yourself—stay in the Word and prayer, create accountability, be intentional about protecting your heart, etc.

Clarify your vision.

"Leading" implies that you are taking people somewhere, and that "somewhere" is (hopefully!) toward the pursuit of a worthy vision. Andy Stanley defines vision as "A clear mental picture of what could be, fueled by the conviction that it should be." If you don't have that clear mental picture, neither will anyone else.

A good vision in children's ministry is characterized by at least three things:

1. It is fully aligned with the overall vision of the church. This is not an option! If you can't align the vision for children's ministry with that of senior leadership, then either it's the wrong vision or you are at the wrong church.

2. It is B.I.G.—Bold; Invigorating; God-centered.

- People want to be part of something that, unless God intervenes, is bound to fail. Be bold!

- People want to be part of something that gets their blood flowing. Make your vision invigorating.

- People in your ministry want something that makes an eternal impact. Keep everything focused on pursuing God.

3. It is shareable. A good vision is one that can be articulated in a clear and compelling way, not just by leadership, but by everyone. Try to refine your vision down to a short, simple, single sentence, and be able to explain it in a clear and compelling way in 30 seconds or less. If you can do this, others will be able to also.

CREATE A CULTURE OF LEADERSHIP.

Many children's ministries have a culture of following. Volunteers are asked to complete tasks—teach a class, run games, prepare curriculum or crafts, lead worship, etc.—and when they are done, they're done. No real leadership is taking place, as they recognize the children's pastor or director as the leader, and they simply follow in doing what they've been asked to do. Many children's ministry leaders unknowingly encourage this culture of following. They simply assign tasks for volunteers to do. Of course, there are literally hundreds of tasks to be done every week in children's ministry, many of which don't have a volunteer to do them. So who does them? The children's pastor or director. This scenario plays out week after week in churches across the country, leading to tired and frustrated children's ministry leaders.

A culture of leadership is one in which leadership is expected, encouraged and shared. But how do we create that culture? Here are a few ideas:

- Think people over program. We need to approach our ministry in terms of investing in people, not building a great program. As we do this, we begin to view potential volunteers not just as someone who can fill a particular role, but in a broader sense—as someone who can grow into a leader.

- Think vision over need. Usually we recruit to big need instead of inviting to a great vision. Followers respond to need, while leaders respond to vision. If you want a group of followers, stay focused on the need. If you want a group of leaders, stay focused on the vision.

- Think long-term over short-term. Short-term thinking is usually about getting things done on a week-to-week basis, which lends itself to a focus on need and program. Long-term thinking is about focusing on an investment in people who will help pursue the vision.

- Think developing over equipping. Everyone must be equipped for the responsibilities they are assigned. But if we leave it at that, then they are only followers. We must also develop leaders, which we'll explore more in the next section.

Note that program, need, short-term thinking and equipping are all important elements in our ministries. However, too often we are more focused on them than on the more important elements.

DEVELOP LEADERS.

Developing leaders is, perhaps, the single most significant responsibility you have as the leader of your children's ministry. A consistent commitment to this investment will reap returns beyond any other investment. But few leaders make this commitment. It is slow. It is hard. It is focused on the few. It is time-consuming. And, probably the main reason, it is something few know how to do.

So how *do* you do it? First, make sure everything already mentioned is happening. You've got to be a leader to develop leaders. You've got to understand what leadership is and have a clear vision for why you are developing leaders. And you've got to have an environment where leaders know they will be valued and able to thrive. These are all part of a process which can be messy, happen simultaneously and require continual adjustment.

Once these things are in place, developing leaders becomes a natural part of the process. Here are a few ideas to develop leaders in your ministry:

- Identify potential leaders. Potential leaders are people who are high in character, consistent, positive, loving, teachable, engaged with the vision, willing to offer new ideas, good with people, good communicators and wanting to do more. From the list of potential leaders, engage with a few who might be willing to be intentional about working with you in a leadership development process.

- Create a plan. With each individual, the investment plan will be different. However, without a plan, it is difficult to be intentional about growth. Get to know the people you will work with, identify their dreams and desires, customize a plan for growth (it might include reading books, online learning or simply regular conversations about specific areas) and help them grow in their leadership ability.

- Use ministry vision for individual growth. You are primarily focused on helping them grow as an individual, but you also want that leadership ability to be valuable to your ministry. So maximize what is happening in your ministry to help them grow personally. This might mean helping them grow as a communicator, which helps them teach kids' church better. It might mean helping them grow in organizational skills, which helps them better manage oversight of a whole department in your ministry.

- Commit to the process. Leadership development does not happen overnight, or in a week or a month or, in many cases, even a year. You must stay committed to the process with those whom you are developing.

- Teach them to develop others. As you develop leaders in your ministry, your ministry will grow. As you teach leaders to develop other leaders, your ministry has the potential to explode. When you have a ministry that is all about developing and being developed as a leader, your ministry will not only grow, but grow in the healthiest way possible.

CONCLUSION

The day that intern walked into my office was the day my approach to ministry changed forever. Though I had heard John Maxwell say it over and over again, the idea that "everything rises and falls on leadership" had never really sunk in. But leadership really does matter in children's ministry, and when we focus on leadership matters, our ministry will change forever.

PULSE: PUMPING LIFE INTO YOUR KIDS MINISTRY

 Greg Baird is the founder of KidMin360. His passion is to assist children's and family leaders to serve kids, parents, volunteers, staff and other leaders to their full capacity.

THE EVOLUTION TO FAMILY MINISTRY

BY **TREVOR LEE**

I went from leading a student ministry of hundreds to leading a children's ministry with less than a dozen children. Some may say that this transition was the opposite of a promotion, but God was leading me somewhere. After serving in student ministry for a decade, I began noticing a trend; students who carried on their faith had several things in common. I'd like to talk about one of these commonality, parents where supporters of their faith. They may not have been an accurate model of their children's faith but their support and encouragement spurred their child's relationship with the Lord. You see, God was leading me to design a ministry that was intentional with not only sharing the Gospel with children but empowering parents to actively participate in their child's faith.

As I discovered, the movement of "family ministry" is not about adding another program but simply elevating the home to be the primary environment for discipleship. Coming from a larger church this seemed like an unachievable goal; I knew how to grow a ministry. My team and I knew programs, events and incentives to get youth into the door but God was calling me to not only grow a ministry by numbers but by an ambitious vision to empower parents to disciple their children. Every Sunday churches come together to celebrate the Sabbath and as they do the children's ministry engages, leads and teaches the youngest members of the church. However, I agree with the argument today that claims that today's model of children's ministry has removed the spiritual responsibility of the parents and has positioned the church to become the exclusive teachers of the faith. This shift in ministry did not happen overnight and to understand where we need to go, we'll need to understand how children's ministry evolved.

HISTORY OF CHILDREN'S MINISTRY

The beginnings of children's ministry came about during the industrial revolution, a time where the socio-economic climate was not friendly to families nor to young children. Before the establishment of child labor laws, children were working side-by-side with adults. One of the traditional origins of the Sunday school model began in the town of Gloucester, Scotland. During the industrial revolution families began moving from the country side to the city of Gloucester, the leading producer of pins. To manufacture these pins children, who had small hands, were needed to properly manufacture and ship these pins. Women, men and children worked up to 15 hours a day, six days a week- with Sunday being the only time off. As such, children were turned loose in the streets on Sunday causing mayhem and opening up an opportunity for the church to step in.

A wealthy newspaper editor by the name of Robert Raikes stepped in with an idea that still to this day is causing ripples.

On Sunday mornings Robert Raikes would venture around town and collect the children for Sunday school. This process repeated itself every Sunday, in the hope that over time the education and moral training would produce a whole new generation of people that can function in society. Sunday school not only focused on poor children who worked and labored in the industries of Gloucester, but advertised the need for universal education. On a typical Sunday children would learn academics, such as reading and writing. Raikes firmly believed that the solution to the socio-economic issues the families faced was education; the ability to read and write would dramatically change the lives of the poor. These early children's ministry classes engaged in hands-on and interactive styles of teaching. It was this level of creativity and focus that elevated Raikes' ideas of Sunday school to the national spotlight.

Raikes desired to solve the social ills of the time through the education and moral training of the children; however as Sunday school generated notoriety the voices of the opposition also rose. One of the largest critiques against Sunday school was the removal of parental influence in the spiritual upbringing of the children. Many in the church, past and present, view that parents have a part in teaching their children the faith. Children's ministry also teaches the faith to the children without the parents involved. Because the parents were not tracking with their children at Sunday school, most of the lessons being taught did not extend to the other six days of the week. Almost 250 years later the church began seeing the need to partner with parents and return to a model that would recouple parenting with spiritually leadership. This is where the return to a "family ministry" model began to pick up steam, before we discuss the steps to starting up a family ministry we need to establish a clear definition.

DEFINING FAMILY MINISTRY

Starting a family ministry, in many ways, is like a hike in the wilderness. If you do not have a clear path or do not have any clue where you are going you are bound to get lost. However, getting lost in ministry can have more implications then ruining an afternoon, it can have eternal repercussions. When we embraced the direction our children's ministry needed to go, we wrote a vision statement that clearly justified our existence. By defining what family ministry is, we can begin taking steps toward living out the vision God has given us. The vision our church has not only defines family ministry in our church, but clearly communicates to our church why this ministry exists.

We sought to cast a vision that expressly commissioned parents as the primary spiritual leaders of their children- and not create another environment for ministry programming. The vision had to embrace our desire to see parents leading the children in faith and not our Sunday school. Our vision is "Family Life exists to empower parents to build their child's faith in God". I do not expect you to copy this exact vision, but understand that in many ways this defines our idea of family ministry. Biblically you will find verse after verse defending the importance of parents being spiritual leaders. The idea of empowering parents was a key element of our vision. We wanted to clearly declare the importance of investing in our parents but at the same time express the truth that parents need to be elevated to a level of authority in their child's faith. At our church, we define family ministry as a desire to continually inspire parents to embrace their Biblical calling of modeling faith for their children. There are deeper desires and focuses of our ministry, but everything depends on the parents discipling their children.

STEPS TO EVOLVING A FAMILY MINISTRY CULTURE

In many ways, I wish ministry was as simple as baking. A little bit of this and a little bit of that, one hour in a oven set at 325 degrees and bam...you got a delicious goody. However God works differently, He likes being original and creating something unique. Family ministry is nothing like baking a cake, but there are some clear elements that can help champi-on a movement to empower parents. As our church explored the real life applications of family ministry I began to notice a fundamental element of success for family ministry imple-mentation: passion. That might sound cheesy but it's true. If you want your church to have an effective family ministry you must have a church, leadership, pastors & parents who are passionate to see family ministry succeed.

- **Lead Pastor:** The lead pastor is called to his/her po-sition for a reason; they are responsible for the vision/mission of the church. Many lead pastors are in the po-sition to guide the church in the direction it needs to go. With the help of others, the church moves in that gener-al direction. Therefore, family ministry needs to be part of the vision and mission of the church. The lead pastor must embrace family ministry as a priority or it will go nowhere.

- **Key Leadership:** Key leadership includes the movers and shakers that become the drumbeat and the de facto voice of the church. They are the elders, deacons, direc-tors, board members, committee chairs, and the non-ti-tled influencers of the church congregation. Family min-istry is not a singular program or a one-time event, it's a passion that needs to surround and resonate throughout the church. Meet with these people of influence and get to know them. Get them connected and encouraged to be a component of this passion for family ministry. With-out these key leaders nothing, I mean nothing, will ever move forward in the church.

- **The Church:** The church needs to embrace family min-istry. Until the church body recognizes that family min-istry is intergenerational it will be just another bullet point on your church's "About Us" pamphlet. This means that single adults serve children, families embrace unre-lated teenagers, and the elderly love the single-parent families. The point is that the church embraces each other as a family, not as a congregation. This can be done in small groups or large groups, it doesn't matter. However, it must not be another program but rather a grass roots desire born out of a passion for family ministry.

- **The Parents:** In most church settings I have noticed that partnership simply implies, "I am the pastor, and this is what I need you to do". This is not partnership, but dictatorship... family ministry does call for an element of leadership but to inspire the parents to lead their children partnership requires dialogue. When we authentically engage in dialogue with parents we establish credibility, this credibility enables ministry leaders to be effective. Unfortunately ministry leaders too often lead the family ministry vision by dictation rather than cooperation. The parents are important to your vision and bypassing important conversations with them can lead the family ministry vision into the ground.

- **Implementation:** Relationship can forward a ministry so far but the events, programs and structural elements all have to align and aim towards the vision. In everything you do as a ministry must properly answer the question: "Does this empower parents to build their child's faith in God?" When the answer is yes then you have proper implementation of the family ministry vision, however if the answer is no or not very clear then go back to the drawing board. You want to create a consistent culture, when you side-step vision or promote ideas in conflict with vision you will quickly get off course.

Once again, this is not a baking recipe; establishing a vision that drives your church and families takes more than that. However, these elements outline clear steps that can lead you to have dialogue and open opportunities to embracing a family ministry vision. When it comes to ministry we need to have a deliberate plan, a plan that is flexible enough for course corrections but clear enough to not get lost.

DEFINE THE OBJECTIVES OF FAMILY MINISTRY

What truly defines a "win" for a family ministry approach? Your answer will make a difference in your ministry and gauge the effectiveness of your vision. The community that your church serves in can vary dramatically; because of this a church must respectively embrace their culture but ensure to speak truth into that culture from where they are at...not where you want them to be. For us, this meant many conversations and good dialogue with our families to pinpoint not only where they are at but how we can effectively lead them to our defined family ministry. After having these discussions and pray seeking God wisdom, we embraced three defined wins:

- **Kids and Parents attend:** We not only desire to see kids attend church regularly but we want to see parents attend too. On an average Sunday, we deliberately have separate adult and children experiences during church. Although attendance is not our only win it is one indicator of what our families prioritize. In many ways, what families prioritize will likely be impressed upon their children. When a family makes church a priority the natural outcome will be a solid attendance record.

- **Families Invite Families:** When a family first attends our church, they check their kids into children's ministry and one of the questions we ask on the registration sheet is "how did you hear about our church?" I am surprised how often families invite families. If families are excited about attending church, they tend to be excited about inviting other families.

- **Parents Utilize Our Resources:** Like many churches we hand out resources and host opportunities to not only support parents but equip them to live out the vision of leading their children in faith. Although resource can vary, the reason we utilize these resources is to help forward our goal. If parents are confused, not using or not accepting the importance of these resources then it becomes noise. Clearly outline the resources you have, educated them on how to use them and inspire them to take advantage of the tools you are sharing.

CONCLUSION

Is family ministry the latest fad in children's ministry? I say not. It is realignment toward more effective children's ministry. I do not want to get into statistics but if you opened God's Word and search the Scriptures you will be quick to notice that family- by relationship or adoption- is the primary vehicle God desired for true faith development. I am not saying that children's ministry or any age specific ministry is wrong, I simply believe that we need to make sure we not only reach children but the families those children belong to.

The start of children's ministry was a positive one; a beginning that sought to make a difference in the lives of children and in the community. Fast forward a couple centuries and very quickly the church began to clench to the role that parents were originally designed to own. With so many models and visions, we defined that family ministry had a inherit desire to empower parents to build-up faith in their children. This does not happen by accident or good intention; our ministry must take deliberate steps to advance a culture of partnership with parents. It is more than just handing out a flyer or a few lines in your vision statement; family ministry is more than that. What family ministry may look like in your church must be modeled and clearly refined to create deliberate objectives. This might be an ambitious endeavor, but remember what is ministry if we do not continually evolve towards the impossible. We serve a God of possibility, and through Christ all things are possible...especially when God is the designer of families.

Trevor Lee currently serves as the Family Life Pastor at Life Community Church. In total Trevor has spent nearly a decade serving children, students and families in a variety of church environments around the Pacific Northwest. Connect with him at trevorlee.me.

CHAPTER 3
KEEPING LIFE SIMPLE
BY JIM WIDEMAN

Life can sure get wild in the ministry. Have you ever noticed how just when you don't think things can get any busier they do? We've all been there, but really and truly busy is a relative term. What's busy to me might not be busy to you and what's manageable to me might be crazy busy to someone else. Whatever your definition of busy is, it is a source of pressure in your life. Pressure is not always bad. It can cause you to grow or it can expose weakness. The more pressure you are able to handle well, the more responsibility and authority will be handed over to you. The bottom line is our worth to the pastors and churches we serve is tied to our ability to handle the craziness and pressures of life and ministry.

I was forced to delegate. Delegation did not come easily to me. When things would get overwhelming, I would think, "Just find someone to help." But it was hard to let go of things I enjoyed doing and was good at to let others do them. It wasn't until I moved to Tulsa that I really had no choice but to delegate. When I started working at the church, it was in addition to the job I was already doing traveling and training children's workers. This was before Southwest Airlines came along, and in those days there were cities where a Saturday night stay was required for the plane ticket to be reasonable. I had no choice but to allow others to help me at the church when I was stuck in another state. It was the best thing that could have happened. It forced me to let others help me. Over the years some of the best lessons I've learned have been from situations I found myself in that made me ask myself, "What am I doing that someone else can do and what do I need to be doing that only I can do?"

Jesus is our help and peace in stressful times. Are you glad you don't have to face life alone when things get complicated? Here's what the Word says: "God is our refuge and strength, an ever present help in trouble." (Psalm 46:1) Not only was Jesus called the Prince of Peace, He is our Prince of Peace. "Peace I leave with you; my peace I give you. I do not give to you as the world gives. Do not let your hearts be troubled and do not be afraid." (John 14:27) John 14:16 tells us, "And I will pray the Father, and He will give you another Helper, that He may abide with you forever." Jesus never leads us into something that will harm us. This Helper or Comforter guides us and leads us to God's perfect plan for our lives. God's plan includes a peaceful life.

Jesus is the master of simplifying life. The laws of the Old Testament were many and complex, but Jesus made it very easy to follow them.

> *"Teacher, which is the great commandment in the law?" Jesus said to him, "You shall love the Lord your God with all your heart, with all your soul, and with all your mind. This is the first and great commandment. And the second is like it: You shall love your neighbor as yourself. On these two commandments hang all the Law and the Prophets." (Matthew 22:36–40)*

Jesus' answers concerning life are always simple, even though it may not always be easy to carry them out. Paul too had a quest to keep life simple. In 2 Corinthians 1:12, he writes,

> *For our rejoicing is this, the testimony of our conscience, that in simplicity and godly sincerity, not with fleshly wisdom, but by the grace of God, we have had our conversation in the world, and more abundantly to you-ward.*

Paul had a heart for following the Lord. He patterned his life after the example of Jesus (see 2 Corinthians 11:3). The devil tried to complicate God's simple instructions to Adam and Eve. He still tries today to complicate our lives by injecting thoughts into our minds.

We must choose to keep life simple! It's our choice when things get crazy.

Sometimes our responsibilities and the pressures of life affect us in a negative way. We see this in the story of Mary and her sister Martha.

> *As Jesus and his disciples were on their way, he came to a village where a woman named Martha opened her home to him. She had a sister called Mary, who sat at the Lord's feet listening to what he said. But Martha was distracted by all the preparations that had to be made. She came to him and asked, "Lord, don't you care that my sister has left me to do the work by myself? Tell her to help me!" "Martha, Martha," the Lord answered, "you are worried and upset about many things, but only one thing   is needed. Mary has chosen what is better, and it will not be taken away from her." (Luke 10:38–42)*

We all are faced with this choice, so to help me keep my crazy world on track, here are 18 steps I use to keep life simple when things are crazy:

1. Set your priorities! You can't keep priorities if you don't have priorities. If you can't name your priorities by number at gunpoint then they are not how you order your life. Arrange

your events, tasks and duties by your priorities. My first three never change. My relationship with Christ, my relationship with my family and my pastor's problems. All other priorities in my life can change daily. I must be willing to make these choices on a daily basis. Could you make a list right now of your top 10 priorities?

2. Keep your priorities in order. As I said above, this is a daily choice. The order of your priorities may be different at different times; this is where your leadership must become intentional. My favorite scripture in the whole wide world is Proverbs 28:2 "When a country is rebellious, it has many rulers, but a man of understanding and knowledge maintains order." Maintaining order is the missing element in becoming a super leader.

3. Delegate to others those things that they can do for you even if it's short term. When you're out of time, use someone else's. There are times I need to delegate something long-term and there are times I do it for a season. Make a list of everything you are doing that someone else can do. I hear you saying "But they can't do it as well as me." I know, I've been there. This is why you use checklists and job descriptions as well as special assignments to get them to do it your way. If you have not identified where you need help and what you need to stop doing, you'll just keep doing what you've always done and have the same results.

4. Use time saving tools. Every job goes smoother when you use the right tools. Here are the tools I rely on to help me keep my life simpler:

- Cellular phone. PDA phone is the best of both worlds, and yes I want an iPhone.

- Timer. (Thank God for Radio Shack!) I use a timer to stay on time and end meetings, phone calls and sermons after the time I have allotted.

- Calendar. You can't manage time without a day planning system. I use a PDA because I had reached a place where my calendar system was a time waster. How did you know that, Jim? Because I have developed a habit that saves my bacon on a regular basis; I account for my time daily as I spend it.

- Voice mail. It can eliminate some memos and even a meeting. A tip to remember—when you can, leave details instead of needing a call back.

- Computer. Where my master calendar is kept. I use a laptop because it helps me keep life simple everywhere. Having a computer with me everywhere helps me meet deadlines, network and brainstorm with others and do things once rather than constantly redo. I depend on a computer so much that I have a spare just in case I need it.

- Email. I use email groups and drafts, so things I say over and over I can send without retyping and those people I send to a lot I make a group. The problem with email is knowing when to talk and not type; it's all about keeping life simple.

- Blogging and websites. Both can be huge assets in communicating with key leaders, workers and parents.

5. Do more than one thing at a time. I try to always make the most of waiting, commute times and meals. All three of these are great times for study, meetings and people development, time to return messages and emails and to make assignments as well as plan. Take something to read with you wherever you go. I even use a hands-free phone so I can type and check emails while I talk.

6. Decide what can be postponed or eliminated. This step goes back to priorities. You are the only one who can determine what's urgent and what can wait. Don't just look at the task, look at the time you have and the time involved. Learn to say no! This is a key skill required to simplify life. I've also learned that a big part of saying yes to urgent and important matters means you MUST say no to less urgent or unim-

portant things. When time is short, I look to managing me first, then others and manage things last.

7. Get creative with your family time. I try to take a family member with me every chance I get. I also try to combine my family time with something else. I go walking with Julie, go cycling with Julie and Whitney, play tennis with Yancy and Julie, go to the movies with my son-in-law and shopping with them all. Call them when you can just to say hi.

8. Schedule a break even if it's only for a few hours when you are at your craziest. Even convicts get time off for good behavior. If I can't go out of town or schedule a massage, I make time to play my guitar, visit a music store, make a Starbucks run or visit a bicycle store. These kinds of breaks are real therapy for me and all take me to a happy place.

9. Be open to change in your lifestyle. Different results require different actions. Don't despise change. Change is not a four-letter word; it's a six-letter word and can be your friend. (Which is also a six-letter word.) When I have to change something that I know is not a permanent change, I remind myself this is only for a short while and I can do this! As with anything else, guard your thoughts and your tongue and line them both up with scripture.

10. Do your homework and see what others do in hectic times. I love to study busy people. I check up on busy people by calling, emailing, reading their books and blogs, networking at conferences or visiting Facebook. I look for new places to learn all the time.

11. Stop and listen to Jesus. I shouldn't have to say this to children's ministers, but make time for the Word! You are the only person who can make sure you stay refreshed spiritually, and that you feed your spirit. If you can't go to church, listen to the CD. Sing and praise God in the car, in the shower and in the craziness of life.

12. When you are tired and busy, don't think—rely on a checklist. I've been saying this since before I got gray hair, "Paper is for remembering, not my brain." I don't try to remember anything that I can know by having information with me.

13. Don't ever quit or make big decisions during the madness. Major decisions and crazy times don't go together. This is a key rule to remember.

14. Don't make people decisions when time is limited. When it concerns someone else, take your time and consider things from every angle. Always treat others the way you would want them to treat you or your kids. Don't let the shortness of the hour keep you from making a wise decision; slow things down and think it through when it affects people.

15. Develop a plan to make next year better. Learn from your experiences. As soon as an event is over I ask my team, "What did we learn? How can we make it better? What do we need to simplify?" Do this while it's fresh on your mind; go ahead and start next year's file.

16. Get feedback from others. A good leader is a good listener. I consult others beforehand, during and afterward and get a cross section of opinions from different perspectives.

17. When it's over, crash! Get some rest. I try to always schedule a break between big pushes. Watch out for too many irons in the fire. Be realistic on the amount of projects you take on. I have learned to get others on board to help limit what I do. I have a group who run outside projects so I don't take on more than I can handle.

18. Do more by doing less. Focus on the main thing. Why were you put on the earth? If God has a wonderful plan for your life, (and He does!) then what is that plan? Focus on your main thing. Focus calls for a concentrated push or intentional actions. What are you doing presently that's keeping you from your main thing? Just because it a good idea doesn't make it a God idea.

If you are serious about mastering the art of simplifying life, you must master the habit of evaluating constantly. Listen to your spouse. Ask the timeless question, "Where's the beef?" Examine and inspect fruit, gains and losses. Evaluate efficiency and look for ways to build systems and streamline efforts. Every experience in your life teaches something. A great question is, "What did I learn today from life?"

Ask daily "What should I discontinue, change and/or add to my life?" Last but not least, look for your next step. God leads us in steps, not leaps or jumps. We calm the crazy and simplify life by walking life out in steps and climbing them one at a time.

 Jim Wideman is a speaker, teacher, author, leadership coach and ministry consultant with over 37 years of hands on experience in the local church. Jim currently serves as the Executive Pastor of Northstar Church in Pryor, OK. Jim and his wife Julie have two daughters and a grandson.

CHAPTER 4

WHY KIDS (REALLY) MISBEHAVE

BY DR. RICK CHROMEY

ot a problem child? Good. Every teacher and children's leader has one. It's God's gift to keep us humble. Troubled children create trouble. The question is how will you react and respond?

Misbehavior is the number one frustration in the classroom. When children act up or out, your defenses go on alert. Disruptive behavior runs the gamut from poking to punching, from whispering to whooping, from playfulness to punishable offenses. In a classroom or children's ministry activity, kids will talk too loud and too much, grab things they shouldn't and ignore things they should and generally keep you on your toes (just to step on them). It's nothing new. From the dawn of education, in some cave dedicated solely to learning stuff, little Bam Bam was breaking his teacher's Stone Age heart by being bad.

KIDS WILL BE KIDS.

At this point it's easy to resign your fate to the problem child. Give in, let up, call off or sneak away saddled with "I'm not meant to teach kids" ringing in your psyche. Or, you can reward good behavior with food, toys and other treats in hopes of turning bad kids good. If you can't beat them, bait them, right? Or, you can revenge misbehavior with punishment. Time outs. Loss of privileges. Loss of rewards. Yet, all these strategies are reactive in nature. Misbehavior happens and we respond in kind. But what if there's a better way?

In my home I have several working smoke detectors. I also have a couple fire extinguishers. Both are useful for fire management. Smoke detectors are proactive in that they continually sniff the air for smoky odors. Often they beep without a fire present. But what do you do when a smoke detector beeps? I bet you don't ignore it! My guess is you figure out the origination of the smoke problem. Sometimes it's a legitimate fire and caught early, no serious damage happens. Sometimes it's merely smoke from Dad burning supper again.

Fire extinguishers are a more serious beast. These canisters filled with foam smother a fire and snuff it out. They're only used when the fire is uncontrollable and the next step is a 911 call. Fire extinguishers are last resorts. They're good to have in a pinch, but most homeowners would prefer they stay unused.

Smoke detectors sniff. Fire extinguishers snuff.

Proactive discipline sniffs. Reactive discipline snuffs.

In reality, most classroom management courses, seminars and workshops deal with fire extinguishers or what to do when there's a problem. Unfortunately, a few of the strategies throw gas (not water) on the problem. The technique doesn't exterminate the problem; it exasperates it!

It's far better to know WHY kids misbehave. It's better to build a smoke detector classroom that's continually sniffing for misbehavior and correcting the friction before the heat and smoke become flame. Sniff or snuff, it's your choice. It's always your choice.

Ironically, biblical insight on discipline suggests a proactive perspective. We've all heard about the "rod" of discipline. Most teachers (and parents) view the rod as a punishing tool (and there are scriptures to back this idea up), but a rod was used primarily to count and correct. A rod separated sheep. A rod's gentle rap let the sheep know of the shepherd's presence. A rod guided and guarded. As the shepherd walked his flock, he used his rod as a moving fence to keep sheep in line. When one misbehaved, the beast got a gentle rap or guiding with the rod. Only if the sheep's life were in danger would a beating come. It's the reason David could sing in Psalm 23 that God's "rod" is comfortable and soothing. The rod of discipline creates security. It's a guide and guard, and if absolutely necessary a torture device. The rod corrects even the tiniest misbehavior. The goal is submission in order to move forward, grow or accomplish a task.

The problem in many Sunday school classrooms and children's ministry events is the teachers and leaders resort to rods of punishment to stop misbehavior. We pull out the fire extinguisher and smother disruption. Such tactics do work, but they also create wet, irritated, frustrated and grumpy sheep. *Punishment always answers the misdeed but rarely, if ever, does it address the reasons.* It's far better to sniff out misbehavior and correct it early, than to let behavior smolder, flame and burn before we act.

Why children misbehave is far more important! So why do they really act up? And what if our fire extinguisher strategies actually make the fire hotter? In reality, there are three simple reasons for misbehavior in all human beings, regardless of age. Learn them and you hold the key to proactive discipline.

BELONGING!

The first reason children misbehave relates to belonging issues. Psychologist Rudolf Dreikurs proposed every human being possesses a "genuine goal" to belong. In every social situation we seek to fit in, commune and feel a part. After all, if we don't belong, it's so long. We check out—mentally, emotionally, spiritually and eventually physically.

Dreikurs theorized when humans don't meet this goal to belong they pursue "mistaken goals" in order to feel the love. Each of these mistaken goals is like rungs on a ladder of misbehavior. The first rung is attention getting or innocuous, often overlooked whiffs of misbehavior. There's friction and smoldering, but no fire yet. The second rung is power plays or attention-getting strategies! We have heat and clear smoke. The alarms are sounding, even though there's still no flame. Revenge is the third rung. Now the power plays, if not resolved, turn personal. Fire is on the floor! Finally, if still no resolution to belonging happens, the person simply gives up. His/her attempts to belong were smothered by discipline strategies that fueled the flame.

These levels of misbehavior—attention seeking, power plays, revenge and resignation—were merely the ripples of the real reason: belonging. So let's get practical. If a learner struggles to belong and tries to flag your attention through low-level misbehavior, how should you respond? Most classroom management courses and books suggest ignoring the behavior, but that's a problem. Will ignoring low-level misbehavior help the child feel like they belong? *Ignoring misbehavior only fuels it. So stop ignoring low-level misbehavior.*

Power plays (and even revenge) are discouraging, but how do many teachers and leaders respond? In reality, we power play right back! We use strategies that embarrass (write names on the board), punish (loss of reward) and separate (time outs). And yet, do such power plays make the misbehaving learner feel more love or less? More like they belong or less like they belong? Now you see the problem.

Dreikurs' theory revolutionized my classroom management schemes. I chose to sniff for belonging issues and then respond, as needed, to help children feel the love and belong. I reacted to attention-getting by proximity. I didn't ignore. I got close. I appropriately touched the child. I called them by name. I gave them a responsibility or role. I snuffed out their belonging issues before they could heat into power plays. And frankly, I rarely see power plays anymore! When a child feels the love and fits in, they behave.

BOREDOM

A second reason for misbehavior is boredom. They're tired of learning because the teaching is tiring. Boredom follows similar paths of disobedience as belonging. First, the learners playfully disrupt and then they power play disruptions.

Here's the kicker: Who has control of boredom? The hard reality is the teacher (not the student) has the power to bore no more. Unfortunately, too many Bible teachers and children's pastors prefer to write their own curriculum rather than use a professional curriculum wired with creative, tested learning strategies. Secondly, there's a lack of preparation and if you don't prepare you will repair. *A bad lesson plan (wired with boring strategies) combined with little preparation is a recipe for misbehavior.* Don't blame your class for acting up! You did it to yourself.

Another factor is attention spans. A child's attention span equals his or her age. Two years old? Two minutes. Five years old? Five minutes. Ten years old? Ten minutes. Actually, most educational psychologists now propose attention spans for those older than ten is still about ten minutes. In other words, we have to keep changing things up. When a child's attention is exhausted, they get bored. And when they get bored, they misbehave.

BELIEFS

A final reason for misbehavior is beliefs. Essentially, we all carry within ourselves a set of beliefs about who we are. Our parents framed these beliefs primarily, but later in life our teachers, pastors and peers also contributed to our frame. As a result, we behave as others have framed us to behave.

We carry this emotional baggage of belief into every social setting. As we interact with others we respond and react according to the frame. For example, many troubled children have been labeled "troublemakers." Many children with problems are tagged as "problem kids." Their troubles and problems now frame who they are.

As a result, kids act out of the negative expectations of adults. When we create rules in the classroom (to correct a few disobedient kids), we actually draw lines for others to act down. If you want to reframe beliefs, you have to set higher expectations. If you expect children to misbehave, they will every time! We behave according to the expected frame.

 Dr. Rick Chromey is a leadership edu-trainer, author and 30-year veteran in children's ministry. He's the author of *Why Kids Misbehave* (digital) and a sought-after speaker in classroom management and positive discipline. Connect with him at rickchromey.com.

CHAPTER 5

RECRUITING FROM A 3-LEGGED STOOL

BY **LARRY FOWLER**

"Thanks! I deeply appreciate that. That's really nice. Thanks."

Eric looked me right in the eyes as he said it. His face showed me he really meant his words.

This young Hispanic man from South Los Angeles was sitting next to me on a plane. As the trip started, we got acquainted; he was on his way to boot camp at the Great Lakes Naval Training Center near Chicago. He told me it was his first trip outside of California, and his first plane ride.

I asked, "Are you nervous?"

"Very" was his transparent answer. "More than that—*scared.*"

47

We ended up having a pleasant, extended conversation about the world, travel, family, and spiritual issues (he was a believer) before we each got in a good nap on the flight. As we were descending into Chicago, I handed him a slip of paper. I was living in Chicago at the time, and I had written my email address and my phone number on it. "Eric, since you said you don't know anyone else here, I want you to have this. If you ever need a friend or somewhere to go on a day off, let me know. I'd be honored to take you."

It was that simple show of friendship that caused Eric's positive response. He, like nearly all people, desired relationships, and he was relieved to know he had one in Chicago—even if it was a brief one formed on a plane trip.

People's faces usually brighten when they are offered friendship. At the rec center where I work out, most people completely ignore one another. But I have found that if I offer a friendly greeting, or encouragement, immediately the other person responds positively. Relationships—even fledgling ones—are powerful.

RELATIONSHIPS IN RECRUITING

When I recruit, I too often forget the potential of relationships. Do you? Maybe you've never even considered it. By the end of this article, I hope you will.

Maybe you are mired in the losing pattern of recruiting based on need. It usually sounds like this:

"We are without a second grade teacher. We're looking for someone to take it each week, but even if you can only serve once every couple weeks, we will be happy to use you." We end up asking for just a warm body, and then too often that's all we get.

I'll get back to relationships in recruiting soon. But first, I want you to consider an image I have found helpful: picture yourself trying to balance on top of a 2-legged stool, proclaiming your message of recruitment. ("Come serve in Kid's Ministry!") You know it is nearly impossible to remain on top of a stool with only two legs. It will tip; you will fall—and your message won't get proclaimed. You need three legs, not two. All three are essential to keep you upright. The same principle is true in recruiting: you need three legs that support you as you proclaim your message. Here are the three legs:

1. The Leg of Purpose or spiritual vision. This is the why of ministry. Carla does this well. As a Sunday morning director in her church, she is by nature a forward-looking, positive person, and loves casting vision. "Come help us change the destiny of these precious kids"—she is fond of saying. The focus is all on the children—on changing their lives forever. "Change the destiny" is the shortened version of her favorite phrase, and her enthusiasm for it is contagious. She has consistently delivered it over a period of time so that her workers repeat it themselves—often. Over the entry to her children's wing she has had written, "Here we change the destiny of young lives." She uses it effectively when recruiting.

She says, "I never recruit to need. Instead, I will tell people, 'The more we have serving, the better we can affect destiny.'" People in her church respond positively. They appreciate her sense of purpose, and as a result, she is well staffed with volunteers. She adds, "In fact, I struggle more with trying to figure out what to have them do when I have more than enough to fill the slots." Wouldn't you love to have Carla's problem?

When you recruit, you will be much more effective if this leg of your stool is firmly in place, and a basis for your message to potential volunteers.

2. The Leg of Position or service activity. This is the what of ministry. Rather than recruiting to the why of ministry, you are recruiting to what it is that people are going to do. Instead of being vision-based, recruiting is volunteer-based.

David's church uses this approach. His senior pastor is a strong proponent of finding your spiritual gift, and putting it to use. As the children's pastor and the largest user of volunteers, David gets the benefit, because he has matched the various positions in his kid's ministry with the spiritual gift assessment.

It's very satisfying for him, because it so clearly aligns with a major emphasis of his whole church, and people are eager to serve where they feel most comfortable. David puts it this way: "Every Christian must find their seat on the bus of ministry. We say all the time around here, 'Get on the bus' and by that we mean find a place to serve. But we also tell people, 'Find YOUR seat—your spiritual gift seat.' Why? Because we believe they will feel so much more fulfilled when they find *their* fit— their seat on the bus."

David doesn't recruit based on need if there is any way to avoid it. "I never just say, 'We need help!' Because what you get when you recruit based on need is a square peg in a round hole." You'll get an administrator volunteering to teach or a teacher volunteering to administer, and as a result everyone— kids, other volunteers, and the individual—are frustrated."

Like Carla, David also enjoys a pretty good success rate in recruiting. In fact, he has a waiting list for teachers. He has found this leg of the recruiting stool very effective and it works great for him.

Imagine blending Carla's approach with David's. You'd have a pretty effective strategy, wouldn't you? I've seen a bunch of effective leaders do that very thing. But let me suggest a third:

3. The Leg of Relationship or personal connection. This is the who of ministry. One of the greatest fears that hinder people from serving, especially in larger churches, is that they know no one in a potential service opportunity. How many people are so outgoing that they will volunteer to work with total strangers? Not many. Think about the flip side: most who do volunteer already have a relationship/friendship/acquaintance with at least one person in that ministry.

So, do you ever emphasize relationship when you recruit? Even if you have the other two legs of the stool in place, people may still be reluctant if they face serving alongside people they don't know.

If you did emphasize relationships in recruiting, it would sound like this: "We have the most awesome team in our middle school department. In addition to ministering to the kids, they have a ball working together; they've become great friends, and they have open arms for more to join them."

In other words, you tell potential volunteers they will find a place to *belong*. We're using that strategy right now in our ministry (Awana); in fact, we've named the recruiting campaign "*You Belong*." If that's a phrase that works for you, you're welcome to use it as well.

I have done this for a while without consciously knowing I was using this approach. When I worked with churches in the Los Angeles area, I had a ministry team of volunteers whom I considered highly gifted and deeply devoted. They loved working together and it showed in their effort. I would sometimes parade them up front at conferences and events, thank them for their incredible effort and then invite others to join them.

I sincerely believe others saw them as effective, and as a close-knit, loving group who had great relationships with one another. As a result, recruiting others to join them started with a position of advantage because of the positive perception that was created.

Do you get this point? A relationship-based approach to recruiting is powerful. In fact, people are many times more likely to say yes to a recruitment plea when it comes from a person with whom they have a relationship—I've already said that. Add to it a call to belong to a group that has the why and what of ministry already in place, and you've got an incredible strategy for recruiting.

The three legs of the recruiting stool: purpose, position, and relationship. When they are all in place you have a solid platform from which to proclaim your recruiting message to potential volunteers.

And Eric? It's too bad he's going to be preoccupied with Navy boot camp. I think I could have recruited him for children's ministry in my church.

Larry Fowler's latest role in his storied 30-year ministry career is as executive director of global networking for Awana and KidzMatter. Larry travels the country connecting with churches and helping them build dynamic ministries to children, youth and families.

CHAPTER 6

THE IO ESSENTIAL FACTORS IN VOLUNTEER RETENTION

BY JOSH DENHART

H igh turnover in volunteers is one of the single greatest inhibitors of ministry momentum. The development and retention of the volunteers *God has already provided* are two of the most important aspects of our pastoral calling. Paul says,

And he gave the apostles, the prophets, the evangelists, the shepherds and teachers, to equip the saints for the work of ministry, for building up the body of Christ (Eph 4:11–12)

It is tough to effectively equip leaders with a transient volunteer population. Here is a common scenario: We recruit someone. We train them. Just as we begin to feel some sense of rhythm, we are informed that "God is calling them to do something different." Constant turnover takes its toll on leadership, shatters organizational momentum and stalls any endeavor.

Patrick Lencioni's *Three Signs of a Miserable Job* states it like this:

> *The cost of job misery is very real. Some studies show as high as 77% of workers are dissatisfied with their work, and that the primary driver of job dissatisfaction is not pay or benefits, but rather the relationship that an employee has with his or her supervisor. Such widespread dissatisfaction kills morale and productivity within companies, and drives up the cost of recruiting, hiring and retaining new employees, all of which takes a huge, and not easily measured, toll on the bottom line.*

Some volunteers stay for a lifetime. Some volunteers only last a short while. If continuity of leadership is one of the single greatest variables in productivity, what factors might be at play when someone is weighing options to quit or stay in a given role? Are there things we can do to ensure no one is a "miserable volunteer"?

THE 10 FACTORS

Over the years, I have gathered anecdotal information about a person's motivation to leave a role, either volunteer or paid. After combing through the deeper details of someone's exit, I found ten common factors in volunteer or employee transition.

1. Compensation
2. Sense of Purpose
3. Work Relationships
4. Appreciation
5. Established Metric for Success
6. Workload
7. Ownership and Influence
8. Use of Personal Giftedness
9. Philosophical Agreement

10. Engaged Managerial Presence

In all of my discussions with someone who has moved on from any role, I asked people to ascribe a value (1-low, 10-high) to each variable, the sum of which provides an aggregate volunteer or employee health score. An aggregate score at or below 75% usually spells danger. Their exit interviews were consistent: one or two of the ten variables had inevitably waned. Though many of the variables may have been relatively high, when one or two variables were uncharacteristically low, the scales tipped, and they quit.

A CLOSER LOOK AT THE 10 FACTORS

#1—Compensation

In ministry we use volunteers. We do not get to pull the seemingly almighty monetary lever to retain volunteers. Money might look like the easy solution, but alone it is not able to overcome glaring deficiencies in other areas. In the absence of financial compensation, we have the opportunity to develop excellent shepherding skills with our volunteers by intentionally investing in the other nine factors. We often scratch our heads when the successful corporate manager making $375K quits their job. Someone's compensation might be at a 10, but it cannot offset other areas found wanting. Money is no panacea.

> *Get Practical: Though compensation is not the most important factor, never forget that it is a factor nonetheless. As volunteers show deeper commitment, develop a stipend program where you include compensation, even if only a small amount. A little extra money can actually go a long way. This investment puts you on your way to developing a KidMin staff team.*

#2—Sense of Purpose

Business leaders may feel they have the elixir of monetary compensation, yet the Word of God holds one of the most important variables at our disposal: heavenly reward and pleasing God. The Scriptures are brimming with the promise of heavenly reward for faithful service unto Christ. As a first century shepherd of God's people, Peter shared, "I think it right, as long as I am in this body, to stir you up by way of reminder..." (2 Peter 1:13). Be a student of the promises and share them freely with your volunteers. Develop a mental storehouse of the promises and constantly remind volunteers there is "... an inheritance that is imperishable, undefiled, and unfading, kept in heaven for you ..." (1 Peter 1:4)

Get Practical: Systematically record scriptural promises associated with faithful service. Communicate these nuggets in winsome and relational ways in person and in writing. The Word of God has power—use it.

#3—Work Relationships

We all know that serving together breeds community. Yet historically, children's ministry has been one of the loneliest places to volunteer and is often devoid of a true service community. As a result, many churches moved from a traditional classroom (two adults serving 40 children) to a large-group/ small-group model (15 adults serving 100 children). Serving with other adults matters. Yet even within these more relationally-focused volunteer models, someone can serve an entire year "next to" another leader and yet not know their first name. Proximate closeness is not equivalent to relational closeness. Facilitating relational development among volunteers takes time and intentionality, but the benefits are profound.

Get Practical: Host quarterly children's ministry volunteer dinners in homes where families can fellowship without 100 children needing help with a craft. Spouses meet, conversations ensue, connections are made and unbreakable bonds form between volunteers.

#4—Appreciation

Effective leaders must never forget to be effective cheer-leaders. Volunteers are sharing a portion of their one life under our leadership. They could be doing something else. I often remind our volunteers that our ministry is composed of 98.7% volunteers vs. 1.3% staff. I let them know that we could not do without them. The power of our appreciation is directly related to the specificity of our thanks. Communicating precisely why we are thankful for a volunteer's contribution is much better than a generalized, "thanks for serving."

Get Practical: The power of a handwritten postcard cannot be calculated. Commit to 3–4 handwritten postcards a week, and you will be surprised at the results.

#5—An Established Metric for Success

Nothing hurts more than when we specifically thank someone for serving and they say, "You are welcome. But I do not know what I did?!" Leaders create environments where volunteers can easily gauge *for themselves* whether they were successful in their roles. If volunteers are conditioned to self-evaluate, they will ask themselves, "Did I pray with any children today? If yes, I was 100% successful in the area of prayer!" We want volunteers to be outcome-oriented and ask themselves, "Did I ask a child a personal question and use their name in a sentence? If yes, I was 100% successful in being a relational leader this week!" By creating **S**pecific, **M**easurable, **A**ttainable, **R**ealistic and **T**imely goals for our volunteers, their feeling of success as partners with God in children's ministry will skyrocket .

Get Practical: Create 3–4 S.M.A.R.T. goals on the back of a leader's name tag. Keep it simple and celebrate the victories you are seeking to measure.

#6—Workload

Underutilization of key volunteers is as dangerous as over-working and burning out volunteers. Every volunteer role must strike a unique balance. Many children's pastors work so hard to recruit a high capacity volunteer only to assign them to a low capacity task that is nonessential and brainlessly boring. On the flipside, too many children's pastors bog down volunteers with roles that require 10–12 hours/week to be successful. Interestingly enough, both sides of the sword will cut off our volunteers' desire to participate ever again.

Get Practical: Simply ask! Volunteers will tell you if what they are doing seems realistic and doable. If it is not working for them, they often have practical solutions to their own problems.

#7—Ownership and Influence

People stay where they have a say. Ownership in a volunteer-led organization is paramount. A leadership style that leverages collective decision-making can seem risky, yet volunteer buy-in is worth it. Through clear vision casting, we are the driving force of leadership, and yet our followers embrace the idea's inception and outcomes as if it were their very own. It is powerful when a group *chooses* to pursue a direction you could have dictated.

Get Practical: Provide forums about upcoming changes and practice collective decision-making, not "Lone Ranger Leadership."

#8—Use of Personal Giftedness

Not everyone has been endowed with upfront, teacher-type gifts. God has distributed His gifts quite broadly. But if your leadership bus does not have seats for a variety of gifts, many volunteers will not last long. We must tap in to gifts of administration, organizing, and cutting crafts, not just the highly specialized skills of relational discipleship. Do we have room for someone who may feel called to serve kids, but does not want to *be around* kids? We need a relational mechanism of evaluation and possible *replacement* of volunteers or they will move on.

> *Get Practical: Simply ask, "Is this role working for you?" and really listen! Provide personality profile tests like The Strengthsfinder. Provide volunteer job shadowing before long-term commitments are made. Implement a "sunset clause," where each volunteer role has a definite beginning (sun rises), evaluation period (high noon), and an opportunity to walk away and try something different (sun sets).*

#9—Philosophical Agreement

Philosophy runs deep. If someone does not understand why we do what we do, they may quickly surmise they are at odds with the basic tenets of our ministry approach. Unfortunately in most cases, we are actually not at odds philosophically—we just fail to communicate. Preemptively showcasing the ministry philosophy in both the overall vision and the small nuts and bolts can make a huge difference. Listen to their questions. Observe their posture. Provide clarification on why we do what we do. We are likely more on the same page than we might think. Communication saves the day.

> *Get Practical: Hold annual vision gatherings to reestablish the Who, What, When, Where, Why and How of your ministry. Communicate clearly in matters big and small.*

#10—Engaged Manager Presence

If there is one factor that can act as the sole stimulant and catalytic agent for bringing a rise in all other variables, it is an engaged manager. A relational shepherd knows the details of their busy life outside the church and watches to ensure their workload is not unrealistic. An engaged leader surveys the ministry to ensure no one is serving alone as a volunteer. An in-tune overseer checks that an area of service is a good fit for how God made a volunteer. A motivational leader consistently inspires with the scriptural promises of reward in heaven. If a volunteer has a diligent shepherd, it is likely they will stay. If they do not have a diligent shepherd, they will either move on to another ministry area to serve (and hopefully find a caring shepherd) or will give up all together.

THE AWAKENED LEADER

How easy it would be if every volunteer had a graph hovering over their head, indicating their "volunteer health score" at any given moment? Yet this takes away the most essential ingredient in this equation: You! The very act of intentionally interacting with your volunteers *is the very thing that will likely keep them around!* Awakening and cultivating your leadership antenna will make you keenly aware of where to invest in the lives of those you have labored so hard to enlist. Keep the leaders you have right now by meeting their needs.

> *Everyone to whom much was given, of him much will be required, and from him to whom they entrusted much, they will demand the more. (Luke 12:48 ESV)*

Our knowledge of these factors is a critical first step. Yet our commitment to action-oriented investment in these areas will make all the difference for the health of your volunteers, the health of your ministry, and the growth of your personal leadership acumen.

Josh Denhart is a full time children's pastor in West Des Moines, Iowa. As a former chemistry teacher, Josh created "The Amazing Chemistry Show", a traveling gospel-centered stage show featuring fire, explosions and foam. Josh is the creator and publisher of "Science VBS".

CHAPTER 7

CHILDREN'S CHURCH ESSENTIALS

BY **DICK GRUBER**[1]

⎯⎯⎯⎯⎯⎯⎯⎯⎯⎯⎯⎯⎯⎯〜〜⎯⎯⎯⎯⎯⎯⎯⎯⎯⎯⎯⎯⎯⎯

'm a children's church guy. Ever since Mrs. Walker compelled me to help in the spring of 1975, I have been serving in some capacity in children's church. I have been a volunteer, a leader and a children's pastor. I have served in small and large children's churches. For a number of years, I have assisted churches as a children's ministry consultant and coach. In that capacity, I have seen just about every kind of children's church imaginable. Most, regardless of style or size, have been fabulous.

Effective children's services include enthusiastic workers, involved children and a healthy, positive environment for Christian growth. These services do a terrific job minister-

⎯⎯⎯⎯⎯⎯⎯⎯⎯

1. This chapter has been adapted from material found in *Cultivating a Cutting-Edge Children's Church* by Dick Gruber, Morning Joy Media, 2012

ing to children at their current level of understanding while simultaneously preparing them for fifty or sixty years in the adult service.

This chapter won't address best practices in children's church scheduling, the value of larger group/smaller group, time spent in family worship settings or the aggressive style of some children's church teams. Over the years, five major factors have risen to the surface that define the effective children's church. These will be addressed on the following pages. The effective children's church is: Relational, Age-Level Appropriate, Inclusive, Spiritual and Exciting. It is a place where you can raise a generation of leaders, raise spiritual awareness and practice and raise the level of parental involvement in the spiritual formation of their own children.

RELATIONAL

Ministry is about relationship. The New Testament record finds Jesus, pressed by crowds, yet giving time and care to individuals. In 2005 I became involved as children's pastor in a new church plant. My daughter Sarah was serving at that time as a children's pastor in Salt Lake City. I called her to share my excitement about our soon coming start-up Sunday. Sarah stopped me and said, "Dad, you tell everybody that kids come to church to meet with each other and meet with God. You are really good at helping kids meet with God, but horrible at giving them time to meet with each other." Imagine my shock in realizing she was correct. With Sarah's guidance, this "children's church expert" incorporated relationship-building times into his children's church. These times included playing board or video games together, creating craft projects or building with Legos. We spent the first 20 minutes of each time together meeting with one another. Kids must have fellowship time at church. Because of the diversity of communities and locations served by churches, this is the only regular meeting with Christian friends many children will experience.

Workers must spend time interacting with children as they come into, and spend time in, the children's service room. Talk to, but more importantly, listen to children. Contact should be made outside of the church time with children each week. This can take the form of emails, home visits or snail mail cards. Include parents in every relational contact outside of regular church times.

AGE-LEVEL APPROPRIATE

An effective children's service will minister to children at their own level of understanding. This is a tall order when many of us serve in a room that includes kindergarten through fifth or sixth grade. Curricula can, at best, meet the needs of a portion of the age levels represented. It is up to the workers to adapt curricular materials to the unique combination of children they serve. My personal rule of thumb is to gear vocabulary and sentence structure to the third or fourth graders while making the visual aspects of my presentation appealing to the youngest children. Do all you can to impact the senses when teaching in children's church. Add involvement of children in ministry functions throughout the service and even the older children will enjoy what is being presented.

Years ago, my friend Bob Hahn was children's pastor in a nearby church. He was in dire need of helpers in his children's church. With little thought given to the scriptural directive of Ephesians 4:11–12, Bob began to prepare the "saints for works of service." In his case that meant 5 through 12-year-olds. His success inspired me to do the same. Soon, both our children's churches became training centers for young ministers. By involving children in age-appropriate ministry positions, we had stumbled onto the philosophy that children's church is preparing these saints for a lifetime of service in the body of Christ. Ministry involvement of the children has become commonplace now in effective children's services.

Keep service opportunities age-appropriate. Younger children may do something as simple as handing out papers, or holding object lessons while you speak. Encourage your workers to involve children in age-appropriate ways when presenting a portion of the service. The older children can operate your technology, serve as a welcome team, lead in worship and even teach lessons. At times I have partnered children with adult or youth workers in order to help them experience success in a ministry assignment. Small successes build confidence in children as they embark upon a life of service. I have literally sat in the back of the room watching as children ministered to other children in church.

INCLUSIVE

This brings me to the next ingredient in an effective children's service. It must be inclusive. An inclusive children's service recognizes that every child has an important role in the body of Christ. This service seeks to welcome every child at his or her level of need and understanding. The snotty-nosed, foul mouthed, undisciplined child is as welcome as the church kid who looks clean, speaks politely and does everything correctly.

A mom once asked me if her son could attend my children's service. I quickly said, "Sure, we welcome every child." She began to weep and stated that the previous children's leader had said that her disabled son was "demon possessed" and was not allowed access to the other children or services provided for kids at our church. This child was not possessed. He was a fabulous boy, created in the image of God. Because of his disabilities, Charles[2] was wheelchair-bound and unable to communicate. He loved our worship and response times. He showed his love by getting excited and making noise as he rocked in his chair. We discovered that our fifth and sixth grade ministers could help him settle down

---

2. Name has been changed.

by simply holding his hand. They were also supplied with a hand towel to wipe occasional drool from his chin. Charles was able to enjoy our service while other children learned servant-ministry.

Inclusive children's services have a well-developed welcome and follow-up plan. Every child is made to feel special as she enters the service environment. The leader must be intentional in training all children to take part in welcoming and making newcomers feel at home in the service. We had a girl in one church who had not been welcomed by other sixth graders. After her first two Sundays with us, she did not want to attend our service. It took some extra coaxing to get her in the door. I then commissioned workers to assist the kids in learning to welcome, interact and sit with all who entered our facility.

No child should be turned away because of race, economic background or behavior challenges. A well-structured, controlled environment helps every child enjoy the church experience. Part of being inclusive is developing a discipline policy that respects each child, while helping him grow in self-control. An orderly children's service becomes a sanctuary of security for each child.

SPIRITUAL

Here's the part that freaks out some children's church leaders. How can a leader make something spiritual happen? What happens if we promote a spiritual happening and God doesn't show up? How spiritual should this service be?

Generally, the effective children's service takes its direction from what is happening in the adult service. You should never become involved in, or promote practices that are not common in the adult service. The big church service has been established by your pastor and will reflect his or her philosophy of ministry for your congregation. Endeavor to understand and live by the pastor's direction for your church. You can occasionally introduce an unusual method or worship practice when teaching children. Keep from establishing these as habitual practices that are in conflict with your pastor's ministry.

With that said, it is highly important that children meet with God on a regular basis. For this reason, worship must truly be WORSHIP. Music chosen must be theologically sound, easy to learn, understandable to the variety of age levels and pleasant to sing. Children must be given opportunity to express their love for God through songs, testimonies, scripture readings and quiet times. Experiment with biblical forms of worship. Involve children as worship leaders. End each service with special time set aside for a prayer response to the lesson of the day.

EXCITING

Notice I did not say fun. The effective children's service is exciting even when it is not fun. Don't misunderstand; I love to have fun in children's church. I love to employ a variety of methodology that appeals to the fun-seeking child. I have always encouraged my volunteers to have fun teaching and interacting with the children. The fact is, some lessons are no fun at all. From time to time, you will need to, for the benefit of the children present, teach a lesson or series of lessons that are more serious than fun. Two examples come to mind: dealing with death and combating inward focus.

DEALING WITH DEATH

On several occasions over the years, children attending our church, or their family members, have died. Some have died after suffering illness while others have been taken in unexpected tragedies. The children's service is a microcosm of the greater church body. As such, children will experience many of the same stresses felt by adults in the congregation. The children's leader must deal with death when it comes.[3]

---

3. One of the best books I've found for helping children with the death of a family member is *When God Became Apparent* by Darren Daugherty

COMBAT INWARD FOCUS

It is very easy for children, like the adults of your church, to become inwardly focused. They will sit by the same friends each week. Without intentional direction from you, they fail to welcome newcomers to children's church. Growing children's churches develop an outward focus in the children they serve.

CONCLUSION

An effective or cutting-edge children's church is: Relational, Age-Level Appropriate, Inclusive, Spiritual and Exciting. I know you can develop these areas in your children's service. Take time to evaluate what you are doing and how you can improve your ministry to girls and boys in the children's church setting. Effectiveness has little to do with your use of technology or the latest fads in children's ministry presentations. It has everything to do with the five items explored in this chapter. Add the latest gadgets and gizmos to this foundation and enjoy a service that will, by its substance, encourage workers to feel as if they have been to church. They may never want to go to the adult service again.

 Dick Gruber has been involved in children's ministry since 1975. Dick is currently the professor of children's ministry at Valley Forge Christian College. Dick and his son, Aaron host Children's Ministry Talk, a regular podcast answering questions from leaders in the children's ministry trenches.

CHAPTER 8

MAKE IT REAL

BY **KEITH FERRIN**[4]

t started several years ago. We would be driving down the street and hear a siren or see an ambulance. Usually it was Kari who would say, "Hey guys. Let's pray for the people that the ambulance is on their way to help." We would pray as we drove—for the record, my eyes were always open!—and then we would continue on our way.

These days, before Kari and I even hear the siren, one of our kids will say, "Hear that? We need to pray." This one application of the Apostle Paul's exhortation to "pray continually" (I Thess. 5:17) has now become something that our kids do consistently—without our prodding. They have connected the words of Scripture with the reality of everyday life.

---

4. "This chapter is one of the nine principles Keith Ferrin explores in his book *Like Ice Cream (The Scoop on Helping the Next Generation Fall in Love with God's Word)*

I could not agree more with Shane Claiborne's quote at the beginning of this chapter. Our faith has to connect with the world we live in. Let's see where this shows up in the Deuteronomy 6 passage we have been looking at:

> *These commandments that I give you today are to be upon your hearts. Impress them on your children. Talk about them, when you sit at home and when you walk along the road, when you lie down and when you get up. Tie them as symbols on your hands and bind them on your foreheads. Write them on the doorframes of your houses and on your gates. (Deut. 6:6-9, emphasis added)*

Sitting at home... lying down...getting up. These all happen at home. But walking along the road? That covers everything else. Talking about the Bible—and our entire life of faith for that matter—can't be compartmentalized to our own homes and Sunday mornings. If we want the next generation to fall in love with God's Word we have no choice but to help them see the Bible's relevance when they are at school, with their friends, on the soccer field, or on their computers.

Without a connection to real life, faith and the Bible will end up being discarded as things that, quite simply, don't matter. That might sound harsh, but the truth is this: The next generation will not waste time on things that don't make a difference to them. Doing or believing something because you are supposed to, or because your parents did it or believed it, is not a good enough reason.

One of our primary jobs in raising and positively influencing the next generation is to help them see and experience that connection. Can that happen in the home, at youth group, and during Sunday school? I should hope so! But if those three are the only places they are connecting to God and His Word, is that enough for them to make a lifelong commitment?

Not a chance.

When I see "when you walk along the road" thrown in the mix, I can only come to the conclusion that God sees the connection between His Word and everyday life as essential—not just a nice add-on.

So how do we do it? During my time as a youth pastor—and now as a parent—I have learned that the most important ingredient for making that connection is to pay attention. That might sound simple enough, but the more that we intentionally look for times when the stories, lessons, truths, and ideas that we have read in the Bible connect to what we see in everyday life, the more likely we are to bring them up conversationally.

And that is huge.

The next generation loves conversation. They are not so fond of getting "taught" something. If they ask the question— teach your heart out.

If you are bringing it up, make it a conversation. There are obviously an infinite number of possibilities, but here are few ideas to get you started:

- Talk about what God's Word says about compassion and poverty while driving to and from serving dinner at your local shelter.

- Discuss money and generosity as you are walking through the store.

- Talk through Genesis 1 while taking a hike or visiting the zoo.

- Spend the drive/walk to school discussing what is coming up in their day—and then pray about it!

- Talk about God's vision for purity while shopping for a prom dress. (And don't leave out God's vision and desire for us to celebrate and have a blast!)

- Insert 3,000,000 of your own ideas here!

A STORY FROM OUR FAMILY

This power of weaving the truths of Scripture into everyday life became abundantly clear to our family because of a man named Clayton Samuel. Kari and the kids first met Clayton Samuel (they always call him by both names) one day while heading to the zoo. He was on one of the corners holding a sign asking for food. One of the kids asked Kari what the sign said and when she told them, they decided to give him some food from their snack bag. The next time they were headed that way, they decided to actually bring something in case they saw him. There he was. This time they gave him the food, but they also asked him his name and how they could pray for him. Over the next year, this scene played out several times. During one of their 20-second chats, Clayton Samuel mentioned that he knew and loved Jesus too. Our kids' faces beamed.

These chats with Clayton Samuel led to many conversations about homelessness. What causes it? What does the Bible say our responsibility is as followers of Jesus? How can we help? One day, out of the blue, Caleb enthusiastically said, "We have extra room in our house. What if everyone who has extra room in their houses let someone who is homeless stay there? There would be no more homeless people!" More conversations...

During one trip they noticed that Clayton Samuel wasn't on "his corner." The next time, someone else was there. Hoping that this person knew Clayton Samuel, they asked where he was. "He passed away three weeks ago" was the response. Silence. Then Sarah quietly asked, "So, he's with Jesus now? And he's not homeless?" Kari said, "Yes. You're right.

Clayton Samuel has a home now. Forever." More conversations ...

It has been almost a year since Clayton Samuel went home. Just last week, we went to the zoo. On the way home, we drove by Clayton Samuel's corner. One of our kids mentioned Clayton Samuel. He's a person to them. Not a "homeless" person.

Just a real, live person. Oh... and they can't wait to see him again someday. To think it all started with a conversation in the car on the way to the zoo.

 Keith Ferrin is a father, author, speaker, and storyteller. He lives near Seattle with his wife and three kids. Oh...and he really, really likes ice cream. You can connect with him at www.KeithFerrin.com.

CHAPTER 9

LEADING THROUGH CHANGE
BY MICHAEL BAYNE

I remember one Monday morning sitting in my office pro-
cessing the previous Sunday. God had been working in some
amazing ways in the ministry I led. We had a new crop of
talented volunteers who were on board and focused. We were
coming up on an event and sign-ups were going well. We had
momentum, and I was kicking back in my chair to celebrate
what God was up to. A few minutes into my private pat on the
back, my pastor walked through the door and sat down. I glad-
ly invited him into my Monday morning celebration. He was
so excited about what God was doing, and he used it to lead
right into this great new idea he had. We all know when your
supervisor has a new idea it probably means new work ahead.
My pastor crashed right into my celebration by dropping the
ultimate change bomb on me. His idea was that we needed to
hurry and add a third service to our Sunday morning plans. In
a matter of seconds I moved from celebrating to third service

panic. New schedule, more volunteers needed, new challenges dropped into my lap, and my Monday morning celebration was now Monday morning anxiety.

In that moment I was ushered into a season of change. I wish I could say I handled the idea of an additional service with joy and effectiveness, but I actually had to work through frustrations that change always brings. Change is always a path for stress and potential chaos. The topic is one we like to read about and think about, but it takes on a whole new meaning when we have to lead through it. Change just can't be ignored or avoided. It comes, even though we hate to deal with it, and if we choose to ignore it, we set up the ministry we lead for loss of momentum and frustration.

Change naturally brings frustration to the lives of leaders even when the change is something we initiated. It just seems easier to establish something and leave it alone. In the middle of every season of change we easily forget the *why* that drove the *what* we are leading through. As you read this, I hope you'll stop and think about the specific change you're facing right now. Take a few moments to process the *why* of what you are pushing through.

When the church was birthed thousands of years ago, after Jesus gave His followers the Great Commission, things started off with a bang. Thousands of people began to follow Jesus. The early church leaders taught with passion and people got to see the power of God through miracle after miracle. The church grew rapidly and had amazing momentum as news about the resurrection of Jesus spread through the city of Jerusalem ... until Acts chapter 6 when Luke reveals the part of church we all know far too well—people bring problems with them! Take a look at what Luke writes.

Now at this time while the disciples were increasing in number, a complaint arose on the part of the Hellenistic Jews against the native Hebrews, because their widows were being overlooked in the daily serving of food. (Acts 6:1)

Growth created a problem! Make sure you slow down long enough to wrap your mind around this truth. As the church grew, the leaders of the church began to see problems arise in this new movement. The problem led the leaders of the early church to a moment of decision. The leaders could ignore the problem or they could invite change into the way things had always been done in order to be more effective. The leaders of the early church put their heads together and empowered other leaders to help solve the issue. They led through a season of change so the church could move forward. Look at what happened.

> *The word of God kept on spreading; and the number of the disciples continued to increase greatly in Jerusalem, and a great many of the priests were becoming obedient to the faith. (Acts 6:7)*

Because these leaders pushed through the needed change, the message of Jesus kept advancing. This is such an encouragement for us today and it reveals a powerful truth. In order for our ministries to be places where the message of Jesus keeps advancing, we have to become leaders who can lead through change. The goal is not to be a great leader or to get recognition for our hard work. The *why* of having the courage to lead through change is so that we can keep pointing the next generation to Jesus.

If you're going to become a leader who can guide people through the difficulty of change, there are a few reminders you're going to have to constantly come back to when the stress that change brings seems to rob you of the joy of leading. I've led teams for over 16 years, and I still forget some of these when I start the process of leading people through another change.

LEADING THROUGH CHANGE ALWAYS DEMANDS FAITH.

Change always brings risk. You can never predict the end result of change. Some work and some just bring crystal clear clarity that the wrong choice was made. Any change you're facing is, at some level, going to require you to trust God to do the work that only He can do. That is faith. We don't lead through change with faith in our own ability. We lead through change with faith in God who has promised to be with us in every season.

LEADING THROUGH CHANGE WILL ALWAYS BRING OPPOSITION.

You never know where opposition will come from when you push for change in your organization, but I promise it will always show up. It always shocks us when people don't respond well. It's like we have change amnesia. Change will usher in an opportunity for people to push back on your plan, so make sure you prepare for opposition by thinking through your plan. Don't get mad because of opposition. Lead people to clarity when opposition comes!

LEADING THROUGH CHANGE WILL DEMAND FOCUS.

Effective change is focused change. Leading through any change demands we don't get off track in the process. Every change you lead through will uncover new issues that exist in your organization. Take note of those problems, because you will get to address them later. But, make sure that you don't get sidetracked and never finish leading through what you started. When you don't stay focused, you just create more chaos for kids, volunteers and parents—a chaos that destroys trust.

LEADING THROUGH CHANGE IS FUELED BY VISION.

If you have any chance of being a leader who leads well through change, you have to be fueled by a compelling vision. The *why* of change matters as much as the *what. When people are able to embrace vision as the heart of change, they are much more likely to move forward.* Some of us only lead through change because we want to please our pastor or our kids. That may last in the short term, but in the end that motivation will crush you and your ministry. Allow the vision of your church and ministry to fuel every change you make!

LEADING THROUGH CHANGE CAN'T BE DONE ALONE.

I don't care how charismatic you are as a leader, you can't lead through lasting, effective change in isolation. Leading through change gives you the opportunity to bring a team around you to make it happen. Your leadership is magnified when you have a team coming alongside you who will join in leading through the change.

LEADING THROUGH CHANGE IS NEVER FINISHED.

Healthy organizations never move beyond change. *You will never be done with the process of leading through change, because it's actually change that brings life to your ministry.* Change keeps things fresh and keeps the vision in front of volunteers! As much as you want to be done with the current change you are leading through, just remember that another change is right around the corner. Take a deep breath and get ready for the next challenge.

As a leader your ability to lead through change will determine how much your ministry is able to accomplish. Our mission is so much more important than any corporation or community organization because we are leading kids toward a relationship with the God who created them. If that mission matters to you, muster the courage to get better at leading through change. Change isn't easy and that's why your team needs you to lead them through the process. Go for it and lead well.

 Michael Bayne is a guy crazy about his family, Jesus, golf, and college football. He is the Executive Pastor at Grace Community Church, Clarksville, TN and the Team Leader at Parent Ministry for Kids. Twitter @michael_bayne, michaelbayne.net.

CHAPTER 10

PLAY THE BALL WHERE THE MONKEY DROPS IT
BY **ROGER FIELDS**

It's not the art of the performance, but the art of the participation. - Leonard Sweet

MONKEYS ON THE GOLF COURSE

In his book, *Play the Ball Where the Monkey Drops It*, Gregory Jones tells the story about the dilemma English businessmen experienced in Calcutta, India. During colonial times the businessmen wanted to play golf in their spare time. But they had a problem.

Monkeys would dash onto the golf course, grab their golf balls and drop them anywhere they wanted. The rules of golf require that any ball moved after it has stopped must be replaced where it was before it was moved. That required the men to chase the monkeys, retrieve the ball and replace it at the spot where the monkey picked it up. That became exhausting and nearly impossible.

So they built a fence around the golf course. That had little effect as the monkeys merely climbed the fence and swiped the golf balls at their whims. They tried trapping the monkeys. But for every monkey they trapped, it seemed three more showed up. The monkeys even seemed to enjoy frustrating the golfers.

The men came to realize the activities of the monkeys were beyond their control. The men were forced to fabricate a new rule: play the ball where the monkey drops it. If the monkey dropped it in the rough, unfortunately, that's where you played it. If the monkey improved your shot by dropping it in the fairway, that's where you played it.

There are forces in life beyond your power. The world is a dangerous, disruptive place. Monkeys (situations in life) will drop the ball in places you can't predict or control. You can quit the game, spend your time trying to chase the monkeys or play the ball where the monkey drops it.

Throughout the Bible ordinary people became extraordinary as they dealt with circumstances beyond their control. They couldn't control the situations they found themselves in. Often they were confronted by insurmountable odds, opposition from enemies and unfair circumstances. Rather than back away from the challenge, they involved themselves in God's plan in spite of what life threw at them.

They learned to participate with God.

WHATEVER WILL BE WILL BE

The main players in the Bible could have tried to remain spectators, merely watching events unfold and accepting whatever outcome occurred. The Doris Day "Que Sera Sera" approach of "whatever will be will be" had to look appealing at times.

- I mean, really, why spend years building a boat while becoming the town laughingstock? Let's enjoy life while we can. Let the flood come and get it over with.

- Why should I try to impregnate my senior citizen wife to start a nation? Can't a younger couple do that?

- So the government job of brick-making is tough and has few benefits. It could be worse: we could be lost in the woods for forty years. Mr. Pharaoh is not all that bad. Let's stay here.

- So what's the big deal with Goliath? Let him rant about God in the valley. We can stay out of his way.

But Noah, Abraham, Moses and David were not content to be spectators. They got in the game. They partnered with God. Jonah, however, was not quite so sharp. He tried to opt out, going for the spectator role. Participating with God to impact the people of Ninevah was not on his bucket list. He ran. A fish gulped him down then regurgitated him on the beach. Jonah got the point. Participation with God's plan is better than trying to watch from afar.

TURNING SPECTATORS INTO PARTICIPANTS

God went to crazy lengths to get people involved in what he was doing. It would have been much easier for God to accomplish His purposes on His own, but instead he involved people. And that's what makes the Bible stories so amazing. Ordinary people did some outrageous things to participate with God.

- Instead of God pre-naming the animals, He wants Adam to do it. Right off the bat, Adam has a job in the garden. No spectators in the garden.

- Instead of God merely corralling Noah's family inside a fence on the tallest mountain, Noah has to build a barge.

- Instead of God giving Goliath a heart attack, David has to trot down into the valley and kill him with a slingshot.

- Instead of God finding a family who already had kids to start a nation, Abraham has to get his aged wife pregnant.

- Instead of God killing all the Egyptians in their sleep, Moses has to confront Pharaoh and lead the Israelites through the Red Sea highway.

- Instead of God sending angels to crush Jericho, Joshua has to lead his people to march around the city for a week.

- Instead of calling down divine healing, Elisha makes Naaman take a bath in the muddy Jordan to get rid of his leprosy. (Naaman was not happy about this method.)

- Instead of sending a killer plague, Gideon has to lead his puny army with torches, trumpets and pottery to defeat the Midianites.

- Instead of sending down fire to burn up the false prophets of Baal, Elijah has to kill them himself after the fire burns up the altar.

- Instead of the angel telling Cornelius about Jesus, as a result of a bizarre dream on a rooftop, Peter has to tell Cornelius and his family the Gospel.

- Instead of dropping sandwiches from Heaven, a little boy has to give up his lunch so Jesus can divide it miraculously among 5000 people.

- And on and on and on. God involved people to do things He could have done without them.

God was, and is, the master at turning spectators into participants. That's His DNA. That's how He operates.

FLASH FORWARD

Flash forward 2000 years and Christians are now spectators.

People come to church and watch the performance. They listen to the music. They listen to the pastor. A few of them serve in a church department. Most sit. Then go home. Adults who attend church have become professional pew sitters. Kids are sitters. Adults are sitters. Everyone is a sitter.

Why?

Maybe it's because we trained them that way in children's ministry. Over the years our teaching styles produce spectators. We talk: kids listen. We show a video: kids watch.

We have taken the public education classroom model and used it to educate—or rather shape—children into a passive audience.

THE JESUS STYLE

But it doesn't need to be this way.

Jesus taught the disciples by doing things with them. He involved them. He gave them responsibilities. He ate with him. He put them on the boat with Him. They traveled with Him. He took three of them with him to meet His father, Moses and Elijah on the mountain. The disciples participated with Jesus in every way imaginable. And in the end, Jesus turned it all over to them. They took it from there.

There were no bleachers. They all got in the game. They played the ball.

If nothing else, our teaching methods should get kids involved. It should turn spectators into participants.

WIRED FOR ACTION

Kids are wired for action. The good news is that kids crave participation. They want to do something. They are not wired to sit still, listen and watch. God did not make them to sit with their chairs upright and their feet on the floor.

The true test of their predilection for doing is their blind willingness to volunteer for anything. The four most powerful words a kid can hear from you is "I need a volunteer." Most kids want to raise their hand and do something, anything. Anything ... but sit passively.

I travel throughout America conducting live events for kids and families in every denomination and every demographic. I have found that kids are the same everywhere. When I ask for a volunteer, their faces light up and their hands go up. For almost 20 years, I have seen this work with hundreds of thousands of kids. It is a universal principle. I would even say law. Kids want to participate.

Think of it.

1. Your most effective teaching method is participation.

2. Kids are prewired to participate.

So the great news is that kids are already wired for your best teaching method: participation. Kids love to participate; participation creates learning. Perfect.

Tell me and I will forget.

Show me and I might remember.

Involve me and I will get it.

But how do you do that? How do you get kids involved in a learning experience? How do you turn them into participants? Any way and every way you can.

- Give kids ways to serve in church. Let them run the sound and video equipment, take up the offering, make announcements and tell a Bible story.

- Pray with them. Help them pray for their parents, friends and neighbors.

- Give them ways to help people. They can help take food, clothing or gifts to those in need.

- Play games with them. Games are rich learning experiences that help kids learn to win and lose, a skill they need throughout life.

- Involve them in skits. Let them play roles.
- Lead them in saying out loud Bible verses and phrases that will encourage and inspire them.
- The ways are endless.

Instill into them that they are participants at every level of life.

EVERYBODY MARCHES

Bob was bored. Sitting in his house with his three kids on New Year's Day, he wondered what there was to do on a day like today for someone who doesn't watch football. Bob Goff decided to do something crazy. He started a neighborhood parade. He invited all his neighbors to join the parade. No matter how simple, they could do anything they wanted in the parade. They could carry balloons. They could dress up. Or they could just walk. They got a parade queen from the local nursing home. The mailman threw letters out. It was a truly low budget, non-exciting, bland parade.

And it was a smash hit that has been running for some twenty years now!

Did I mention Bob made one rule? Nobody was allowed to watch the parade. He invited all of his neighbors to march in the parade but asked them to close their windows if they decided not to participate.

The rule: everybody marches; nobody watches.

THERE ARE MONKEYS

Kids need to know that life can deal them some twists and turns. Monkeys will drop the ball in places they cannot control. Circumstances will seldom be fair.

Finances collapse. Sickness happens. Families split. Relationships spoil.

But they do not need to try to opt out. They can participate with God and go forward. They can play the ball where the monkey drops it. They will discover that the game is worth it.

 After having planted churches in Kentucky and Florida, Roger Fields launched Kidz Blitz Ministries in 1996. Roger authored a variety of Bible resources and curricula, most recently Plus+, a curriculum add-on. He writes for K Magazine and the KidMin Mashup, an online hybrid of children's ministry thoughts.

CHAPTER II

THE BIG BOX OF POTENTIAL
BY MIKE JOHNSON

When I think about recruiting volunteers, I think of a big yellow box with the word "Potential" emblazoned across the top of it (*Why is the box yellow? Because yellow makes me happy, and when it comes to recruiting volunteers, I try to envision as many happy things as I can before I begin*). When I pull out my flashlight and peek inside of this cheerfully colored box, I find every person who is a part of my church, all of whom fall into one of four distinct groups.

The first group is an exuberant bunch. Every person in this group is wearing a t-shirt and a hat that says, "*I LOVE KIDS!*" These awesome folks are jumping up and down with their hands raised high, yelling at the top of their tiny little lungs, "Pick me! Pick me! Kids are my life! Please, pick me!" I love this group of people because they often come prepared with their own "Object Lesson Tool Kits" and they are always equipped with their own snacks.

The second group of people is milling around and when they notice there is a light shining into the box, they glance up at me, casually wondering why I am staring at them. These people are somewhat interested in volunteering in children's ministry and may do so if they are asked very nicely, but they are definitely not as enthusiastic as the first group. If left alone, the people in this second group will continue going along their own merry way and do nothing for me.

The third group in this box consists of people who are wandering aimlessly. These people are totally clueless that I am standing there watching them and that the lid to the box is even open. For this group of people, volunteering in children's ministry is not even a blip on their radar. In fact, they are probably totally unaware that a ministry for kids actually takes place at their church *(or for that matter, that people even volunteer in their church at all)*.

The fourth and final group of people is those who, the moment I take the lid off the box, scamper into the dark corners of the box trying to hide. These are people who, for some reason, see me as a threat to their normal everyday lives of happiness and bliss. These people are aware of the children's ministry at their church and have even heard about volunteering before, but they are definitely NOT interested. The people in this group will avoid eye contact with me at all costs.

As I use my flashlight to look into this box, I quickly devise a strategy on how to recruit volunteers from the people inside. Within this strategy I decide that my wisest move is to focus my recruiting energies on the first two groups mentioned because they will make my recruiting task a whole lot easier and possibly even fun *(two words not usually associated with volunteer recruitment)*.

What about the last two groups? Well, I will *try* to get them involved by either calling them (*but only at a time when I know they're not home so I won't get rejected in person*) or typing up a sincere, heartfelt email and quickly clicking the send button. Beyond that I won't give them much effort because, quite frankly, I hear the word no from them more than I hear the word yes. And since I don't like the indigestion the word no gives me, I quite effectively push these two groups out of my consciousness. When I do this however, I am faced with a couple of big problems. The first problem I face is that there just aren't enough of the "Pick me, Pick me" people from group one, or of the people who "may serve" from group two, to cover all of the areas I need covered. The second problem I face is that, as a church leader (*and if you work with kids, you ARE a church leader*), God has commanded me to not only involve those who *want* to volunteer, but also to involve those who *don't want* to volunteer. Now, I realize this is a terrifying statement, so before you hyperventilate about what this could mean for you, let me explain why I believe this is so.

In the book of Matthew, a Pharisee came to Jesus and asked Him which commandment of the Law was most important (Matthew 22:36–39 NIV). Personally, I think this is a great question (*even if the motives of this Pharisee weren't the purest*). After all, my inquiring mind tells me that if there is ONE thing God wants me to be doing above ALL other things, let me know what that one thing is so I can be sure I am doing it! As the Pharisee waited, Jesus told him that there was not just one, but two important commands (*reasonable enough*). The first and greatest command is to love God with all your heart, soul and mind. The second one, which is like it, is to love your neighbor as yourself.

There you have it. The Top Two. The Twin Towers of Power. Two Beacons of Light that will guide people on the obedient path of growth God desires for every believer, a path that you and I are commanded to help put people on. Nice and simple, right?

Oh, but wait a minute ... maybe not so much. What was that thing about loving your neighbor as yourself? That's a command I've discovered that makes people nervous, and when people encounter a command that makes them nervous, they usually try to sweep it under the rug and casually act like it's not there. The bad news however is that when people ignore and disobey this second command, they will not grow spiritually as God desires. Take a look at this scripture with me:

> *Then we will no longer be infants ... Instead, speaking the truth in love, we will grow to become in every respect the mature body of him who is the head, that is, Christ. From him the whole body, joined and held together by every supporting ligament, grows and builds itself up in love, as each part does its work. (Ephesians 4:14–16 NIV)*

In this text, Paul infers that all baby believers should desire to grow and become mature under the head of Christ. In real life, babies are cute and cuddly—for a while. Soon, however, we expect these babies to grow up. We want them to assume responsibility for themselves and become fully functioning members of the family. This is true not just in physical life, but in spiritual life as well. Paul says that as a member of God's body, we must grow and mature so we can assume responsibility for ourselves and become functioning members of His family. To make this happen, Paul says we must grow and build ourselves up in love. Love for whom? Love for the very ones Jesus commanded us to love—God and others. When we merge the divinely inspired words of Paul with the words of Jesus Christ, we discover that in order to grow in Christ, each of us must grow and build ourselves up in our love for God AND each of us must grow and build ourselves up in our love for others. But that begs the question, *"How* do we grow and build ourselves up in this love that God desires for us to have for Him and for others?" Paul gives us the answer. We grow and build ourselves up in this love as we WORK. This, my friend, is the hard part. We must work at loving God (*through studying the Bible, through prayer, through obedience, through church attendance, etc.*) and we must work at loving others (*through acts of kindness and service*). When we do this, God promises us that we will grow and become a mature part of the body of Christ and that He will use us to do His work.

All right, so at this point you may be asking, "What does this have to do with my recruiting of volunteers?" I have a simple answer: Everything! Let me explain. If you truly believe people only grow and mature when they are loving God AND loving others, then it is your responsibility to help them accomplish both. Your job is not to do the work of the ministry all by yourself; your job is to give the ministry over to God's people so they can become mature as they serve. In a very real sense, you both administer and minister. You are to organize and provide opportunities where people can work at loving God and also work at loving others! Your job, as a children's leader, is two-fold. Bring children into a growing relationship with Jesus Christ and bring to maturity the leaders who serve alongside you. In God's eyes, one is not more important than the other. They are equal. Someday I believe we will all stand before God and be held accountable for the children He placed in our care, but I also believe we will be held accountable for the adults He put in our church whom He wanted us to help grow and become mature by getting them involved in serving others. When you ask a volunteer to serve, you shouldn't go to them, hat in hand, asking them to do you a favor by serving in the children's ministry. Instead, you should go to them boldly telling them that you want to do them a favor by getting them involved. When you ask people to volunteer, you should not feel guilty about putting them out, or about bothering them. Instead, you should see their lives as your responsibility, given to you by God, to grow and mature through service. You should now say to each person, "I love you enough to keep asking you to serve over, and over, and over, because I know that if you don't serve, you won't grow. And I love you too much to let that happen." When you develop this attitude, you will see recruiting in a whole new light.

Understanding this, I think we can all agree what a privilege it is to be a children's leader. You have been chosen by God to have the greatest opportunity to help people mature in their walk with Christ because you have been afforded the place with the greatest need for people to be serving in the church: children's ministry! We should rejoice in the fact that God has given you and me the privilege of being involved in the maturation of so many other believers. What a legacy we will leave! So what are you waiting for? Get out there and recruit! And by all means, don't forget your flashlight. Some of those corners inside the yellow box can get pretty dark.

 Mike Johnson is Global Children's Pastor of Fellowship Church. In that time, he has seen FC Kids grow from 150 to over 4,000 children at 10 Fellowship Church campuses. Mike is the Executive Producer of Elevate resources on ElevateAtChurch.com and LeadershipForKids.tv.

CHAPTER 12

NO COOKIE-CUTTER CHILDREN'S MINISTRIES

BY **LYNDA FREEMAN**

I f you are reading this book, you are likely a children's ministry worker, possibly part of a paid staff at your church, but more likely a volunteer with a heart for effective children's ministry! You read books and blogs, attend conferences and try to get all the ingredients right and yet, your children's ministry does not look like the children's ministries you read and hear about. You see churches around the world where their children's ministries are alive and growing and you look at your church and wonder how to get there. You try to implement the things you have learned and while some of it may work, you are often left wondering why your ministry doesn't look like what you've read and heard about.

There is a very good reason for this—there are no cookie-cutter children's ministries. What works in one church may or may not work in another. And, while there are components that are essential for every children's ministry to be effective, there is no secret recipe where if you make sure you include each ingredient, you will be guaranteed an effective children's ministry. I enjoy cooking and discovering new recipes is so much fun for me! I know if I find a recipe, I may like it exactly as it is, but I will probably need to change this, add that or take away something else. For example, when I was a child, my grandma made the most amazing sour cream cookies. They were easily six to eight inches across. She always put one raisin in the middle of each cookie—which I quickly removed before eating. I make the same cookie, but put a dried blueberry or cherry in the middle of each of my cookies and absolutely love them!

Children's ministry is like cooking. Take a recipe, but be willing to replace ingredients that do not work with ones that will make your ministry more effective for your church. There are several main ingredients for effective children's ministry, one of which is to definitely understand your church's history, community and culture.

Too often we tend to think that children's ministry is just comprised of churches and children, which, technically, it is, but our churches—and our children—are not identical. Our communities are different. Our people are different. Our histories are different. Our cultures are different. What works in one church may or may not work in another. And, while there are components that are essential for every children's ministry to be effective, there is no secret recipe where if you are certain to include each ingredient, you will be guaranteed an effective children's ministry.

So, what do you do to help your church's children's ministry be as effective as possible? Well, while we can't all follow the exact same recipe, use the exact same cookie-cutter and expect our ministries to all be successful, we can discover our own unique recipe tailored to fit our unique community and people and then set about to implement our own, uniquely effective ministry that impacts the children and families in our own church and community!

Before you can begin to design your unique recipe for children's ministry, you need to understand your own church's history, community and culture. What is your church's history?

A church in the town where I grew up recently celebrated their 150th anniversary. Over those many years, decisions had to be made in order for the church to remain effective in its ministry. Some decisions enabled it to be more effective, while others did not. Currently they are a church of around 250, many of whom were children in this church and are now raising their children in the same church. I attended this church as a child; in fact, the first place I ever served in children's ministry was at this church. Their history can be a positive thing as it contributes to a strong sense of ownership and desire to serve, but it can also make it challenging as the people do not always understand how the things they did as children do not necessarily still work for kids today. It can also create an atmosphere of church politics where these same families think they are the only ones who should say what happens at their church, which can, of course, destroy a ministry's effectiveness.

My husband, children and I lived in Northern California for a number of years. I was the children's director at a church that was just a few years old and had over 1600 people in it. This church had more of a challenge getting people to take a sense of ownership and service, but they were much more willing to try new ways of doing things.

What is your church history? How does your unique history benefit and bring challenges to your ministry? It is important to understand your history and how it affects your ministry.

Along with knowing your church history, what is your community and culture? The first church I mentioned (let's call it

"Church A") has been serving in its community for a long time, but while it has a long history with its community, this community has definitely changed significantly, even in the last forty years. When I was a child, I lived in a house literally across the street from this church. The families on my street owned their own homes, and most of the moms stayed home with the children. Now the majority of those same homes are rentals and many are single parent families. Even in families with both parents living in the home, most have moms who work out of the home. My community used to be a quiet, little farming community with a Norman Rockwell Main Street. It no longer looks the same. Many of the stores on Main Street aren't even in business now. This town is 13 miles from the second largest city in Michigan and single parents from the city have moved here to find inexpensive housing and get out of the city. The community is not the same. The culture is different, too.

Let me share with you an example of what I'm talking about. A number of years ago I led a training for a church (let's call it "Church B") about sixty miles from Church A. Both churches were utilizing the same mid-week children's club, but Church B had a culture and community entirely different than Church A. Church B was in a mostly upper-middle-class community. Most of the children attended private school and were very academically inclined. Church B had a much larger budget than Church A did, so they were able to purchase journals and awards for each of the children in their club program. The children from Church B loved writing in the journals and their parents wanted to save the journals.

Church A was different. As I've mentioned, this church's community is made up largely of single-parent homes. The children attend public school, and while children from single-parent homes who attend public school can be motivated to learn and excel, in this case many of these children struggled to read and write. Some of the 5th graders didn't even know how to spell their own last names or know their own addresses. The parents were not involved and really did not care if their children wrote in a journal or not. The children definitely did not want to write in a journal— it was too much like school for them.

Two communities. Two churches. Both churches had a love and passion for their children's ministry and truly wanted to make a difference in the lives of the children in their church and community. But, what worked for one church did not work for the other. If Church A had continued to try to make their mid-week club work as Church B's club worked, it would have resulted in frustration for the volunteers and kids. The recipe for mid-week club was not the same for these churches. If Church A wants to effectively reach this changing culture of single parent, lower economic families, they cannot expect to do things as they did in the past.

Understanding your own church's unique history, community and culture does not put limits on your ministry, quite the opposite as it frees you to plan more effectively. If you are able to identify your history, you will know if you have generations committed to serving, but who need to be encouraged and educated as to what effective ministry looks like and how it can help them reach the children in your church and community or if you have people who are willing to try new things, but who need to understand the joy in serving.

Understanding your own church's unique community will help you be able to better identify, understand and engage with the people in your church and community.

Understanding your own church's unique culture will help you be able to see more clearly where you may need to tweak your curriculum and programs or how you might be able to make them more engaging and challenging.

What is your community and culture like? Take some time today to think about the unique history, community and culture of your church and the strengths as well as the challenges they bring to your children's ministry. Before you can be genuinely effective in your ministry, you need to understand these three things and how they impact your ministry.

 With 40-plus years of experience, Lynda Freeman has served a children's director for churches of 1,600 people—as well as in churches of 100 people. Lynda has been a consultant for Gospel Light, Group and ZonderKidz/Big Idea, ZonderKidz/Promiseland. Connect with Lynda at aboutthechildrensdepartment.com.

CHAPTER 13

DISCIPLING CHILDREN

BY TAMERA KRAFT

M ost children's ministers concentrate on teaching great lessons in creative ways, but they may miss an important element, one that will cause their students to become lifelong disciples of Christ—discipleship.

Paul is prepared for children's church every week. The children are excited and can't wait to see what he has planned. They have fun playing the elaborate games. They ooh and ahh over the Gospel illusions and creative object lessons. They love the motions to the activity songs. And they learn from the illustrated Bible stories.

Paul puts in hours every week to have an effective program, but he's frustrated because the students in his children's ministry don't really grow spiritually. Week after week, they come and enjoy themselves, but he doesn't see a change in their lives. He doesn't seem to be making a lasting impact upon their lives, and he doesn't know what to do about it.

Jim also uses games, Gospel illusions and creative teaching techniques, but the children in his ministry are growing spiritually. Brittany's mom came to him last week to thank him. Brittany went to her mom after being convicted in children's church for being disrespectful and asked her mother's forgiveness. Tommy led four of his classmates to the Lord and brings visitors almost every week. Kyle asked Jim last week if there was anything he could pray with him about. He told Jim that he felt led by God to pray for him every week. When it's time to pray, children swarm up front to pray for one another.

What makes the difference between Paul's and Jim's ministries? They both do pretty much the same thing in their children's services. They spend the same amount of time preparing and praying. But there's a major difference in the students. Paul entertains the children; Jim disciples the children.

You might wonder how Jim manages to do this. It's not difficult if you understand that we are called to be a part of the body of Christ, not only as adults but also as children. I've heard it said that children are the church of tomorrow. But that's not true. They are the church of today, and if they are equipped, they will become the church leaders of tomorrow. A children's pastor's primary responsibility is to equip the students under him.

Ephesians 4:11–12 (NIV) says, "It was he who gave some to be apostles, some to be prophets, some to be evangelists, and some to be pastors and teachers, to prepare God's people for works of service, so that the body of Christ may be built up."

A pastor's primary job is not to preach, but to prepare God's people for works of service. In other words, a pastor's primary responsibility is to disciple his congregation to do ministry. If that's true, then a children's pastor's primary responsibility is to disciple or prepare children to do ministry.

Here are some of the steps you can take to disciple the children in your ministry:

Disciple children in prayer. Teach your children to pray. Then let them have opportunities to pray. Too often we let children pray, and we comment on how cute their prayers are. When we do that, we reduce their prayers to entertainment. We should be teaching children how to reach heaven with their prayers. We should be encouraging them to pray every day, and we should give them something to pray about.

When I need healing, I ask children to lay hands on me and pray for my body. I teach them scriptures to pray over me. When I need encouragement, I ask children to pray for me. When I need wisdom, you guessed it, I ask children to pray for me. I teach them how to pray, what scriptures to use, and then I ask them to pray. I don't ask them to pray because it's cute. I ask them to reach heaven for me.

If we want children to pray effectively, the first step is to teach them how. One resource I've found very helpful in teaching children to pray is the magazine *Pray Kids*. This magazine is published by *NavPress,* and every issue is written to disciple children to pray. These magazines come in bulk, so you can order enough to place in the children's hands.

After teaching the children, give them opportunities to pray more than a few words at the beginning of children's church or offering. Ask your students for prayer requests, and assign other students to pray for them.

If you have a missions program your children's ministry supports, let your students learn about the missionaries and their prayer needs, and then lead the students in prayer for them. You could also get Children's Prayer Maps for free from Every

Home for Christ in Colorado Springs, Colorado, and encourage the children to pray for a different area of the world every day.

Another way you could give your students an opportunity to pray is to encourage them to choose a leader in the church to pray for every day. Have the students go to the leaders and tell them they are praying for them. The students could ask the leaders they've chosen for specific prayer requests each week.

Schedule prayer walks, and take a group of students for walks around the community where they can pray for their neighbors, their schools and their cities. Some school districts will even allow students to come inside the schools to pray before or after school hours.

Disciple children in evangelism. An important part of being a disciple of Christ is to share our faith with others. We expect our students to tell their friends about Jesus, but we don't equip them with the tools they need. Students must be taught how to witness if they are to share their faith effectively. Spend some time teaching them to share the message and what scriptures to use. Give them illustrations to use when they witness.

One easy tool to help children learn to witness is the witness bracelet. You can purchase these or have the children make them. Just like the wordless book, they use colors to convey salvation. Yellow represents heaven where God lives and wants us to someday live. Black represents the sin that stops us from living with God in heaven. Red is the blood of Jesus that was shed for our sins. White means that, if we ask Jesus to forgive us, He will cleanse us as white as snow. Green means we need to grow in our faith. After they learn what the colors mean, have practice sessions where your students practice witnessing to each other. Then encourage them to wear the bracelets everywhere they go so they'll always be ready to share the Gospel.

There are many places you can go to give children an opportunity to share their faith. You can have them help with a benevolence ministry, or take them to a nursing home, or you can take them to the park or playground for a day, instructing them to look for opportunities to witness.

Disciple children in service. Many in the church have the habit of telling children over and over to sit and be quiet until they're eighteen years old. Then when they reach adulthood, the same people will complain that all they do is sit in the pews and listen. If we are to disciple a generation to serve God, we need to start when they are young.

Think about the things that need to be done in your children's ministry. Do you need someone to run the sound? Train a group of children to do it. Do you need people who are gifted in helps to take attendance, check children in, set up chairs and tear down after church? Again, train children to do it.

The opportunities for children to serve in the church are only limited by your understanding of how much a child is capable of doing. I have used students for sound, video projection, registration, leading praise and worship, praying for others, skits, object lessons, puppets, monitors and many other things. I've also used students as greeters and for follow-up on new students. I've even had 11 and 12-year-olds preach for me in children's church. You heard me right. They preached, and they did a great job. Those children are now adults who are in full-time ministry.

An amazing thing happens when you disciple and release children to minister during your children's services. Your need for workers greatly decreases because your students fill that void. At one point, you may find that to have a large program, you only need one adult or teenager for safety reasons and instruction because your students have everything else handled.

There are other areas that students can be discipled in also. The only limitations are the ones we choose to place on our children. When they are discipled in ministry, something amazing happens. Children grow closer to God. They learn to listen for His voice. They learn that God can use them. He has a plan for their lives. So which are you doing? Are you entertaining children or are you discipling them?

Tamera Kraft founded Revival Fire for Kids Ministry in 2007 to equip children's ministers through consultation and workshops and minister to students through Fired Up Kids Krusades. She was a children's pastor for twenty years at two separate churches.

CHAPTER 14

WHO'S YOUR PAUL?

BY **JENNY FUNDERBURKE**

"**E**very leader should have a Timothy, a Barnabas and a Paul in his or her life." My pastor made this statement to my KidMin leadership team a few weeks ago and it was an "a-ha" moment for many in the room. As we serve, it is pretty common to have a Barnabas, a peer who offers encouragement and accountability. God often sends a Timothy, someone who we are investing and pouring into. However, we too often miss out on having a Paul. A Paul is someone who is investing in your life and someone who is coaching you to be better.

For some reason, in the KidMin world, we tend to isolate ourselves. We may read books or blogs, but we aren't quick to connect with others or to seek out help. We know we need it! Maybe it's due to the tyranny of the urgent and the needs of the ever-approaching Sunday, but we tend to be lone rangers.

I know that's how I was until just a few years ago. I was content to exist in my own little world, but I was also pretty stuck. I was stuck in my way of doing things and stuck in my limited way of thinking. I knew I was stuck but really didn't know what it would take to get unstuck.

In 2008, I had the opportunity to participate in Jim Wideman's first ever Infuse mentoring group. Have you ever gone into something and expected it to be a good thing, but God turned it into something that was a game changer? Infuse has been that for me, but even more specifically, the mentoring relationship that I developed with Brother Jim had a dramatic impact on me and my ministry.

I quickly became a believer in the importance of having a Paul in my life. I also became a loud champion that this should be a non-negotiable for all children's ministers who want to grow personally, so that they can make a greater impact for the Kingdom.

WHY WE NEED MENTORS

I love that God never calls us to do ministry alone. He gives us people to serve alongside of, and I believe He also gives us people to coach us and make us better. Let me ask you this: are you everything God wants you to be and do you know everything that you need to know so that your ministry can be all that God wants it to be? I'm assuming that you, like me, would have to answer that with a big fat "No." So, the next question is, "What are you doing about it?" See, if you're like me, you likely don't even have a great grasp on what you don't know or where you need to improve.

But what if you had someone who could see those things? What if you had someone who cared enough about you to encourage and celebrate the wins with you, but will also stretch you by challenging your weaknesses?

This type of scenario is described by Spencer Click, Associate Pastor of Children's Ministry and Ministry Operations at Bethel Temple in Hampton, Virginia and a fellow member of Infuse. "I had recently been let go from a position. I was hurt by the manner in which it was done. I called my mentor, whom I also consider a close friend, looking for someone to pray with me. He lifted me up and prayed for me. And then at the same time, provided a laser-focused assessment of what had gone wrong with the job. It was spoken in love, but was so amazingly blunt that it had a lasting impact in my life and ministry."

A good mentoring relationship is not one in which the mentor just tells you how wonderful you are. Their role is to be encouraging, but even more so to encourage you to be what God has called you to be. They "speak the truth in love" (Eph. 4:15). And yes, they will also be your biggest cheerleaders.

WHAT TO LOOK FOR IN A MENTOR

In 1 Corinthians 11:1, Paul says, "Be imitators of me, just as I also am of Christ." As you seek a mentor, you want to find someone who you don't want to become a carbon copy of, but who is doing things in life and ministry that are worth imitating and learning from.

First, you want to seek someone who is genuinely following Christ. I believe that you can learn something from anyone, but this relationship should be so special that you should entrust it to someone who is in step with God.

Second, determine what it is that you want to learn. You want to seek a mentor who is experienced and highly capable in the areas in which you want to grow. Who do you want to be like when you grow up? What skills or traits are missing in your repertoire that you would love to learn?

Additionally, you want to find someone who is willing and able to invest in you personally. A mentor relationship at its best will go beyond formalities. It will be based on relationship. This was the component that made Infuse so special. Brother Jim took the time to get to know and to care about each of us as individuals. Make relationship a high priority. Your mentor needs to be someone you genuinely like and will look forward to interacting with.

Finally, you'll have to find someone who has the time. There are individuals out there who have so much to share, but are in a season where they just don't have the capacity. And that's ok. You can still learn from them; it just might not be in this mentoring type of relationship.

HOW TO FIND A MENTOR

So once you know what you're looking for in a mentor, how do you find one?

You may want to try one of many coaching groups that are available today. I recommend Bro. Jim's Infuse (jimwideman. com/infuse.html), but there are many options. The Celera Group (celeragroup.com), Kidology (kidology.org) and other organizations also offer coaching options. If you choose to invest in any of these options, make sure you do your homework to ensure that the format, relationships and expectations are a good fit for you.

A coaching group may not be the best option for you at this time. You may want to seek out another leader within your church whom you feel God is using in mighty ways. There may be a children's pastor in your city or state you could reach out to. Maybe there is someone you have really learned from online who might be a possibility.

God has someone for you to learn from. Your job is to seek them out and to not be afraid to ask.

HOW TO MAKE IT WORK

After you find a mentor, the next step is figuring out what the relationship looks like. Determine what you want to accomplish and how you are going to communicate. Every relationship is going to be unique. You need to decide what best fits you and your mentor.

You and your mentor should determine what the format will be and what materials or topics to cover. Some mentor relationships are more intentional than others. Some just discuss life, while others have a strategic plan of books to read or other content to walk through together.

Sara Richards is the Kids Pastor at Church of the Open Door in Minnesota. Sara also participated in Infuse and says, "In order to make any mentor relationship beneficial, you have to work at it. It takes time to get to know your mentor and for your mentor to get to know you. I also had to be willing to trust and follow the advice of my mentor, which isn't always easy."

DON'T GET IN YOUR OWN WAY

At some point in developing a relationship with a mentor, you have a decision to make. Are you more interested in making yourself appear to have it all together to impress your mentor? Or are you more interested in being open to the needed changes he or she can help you work through?

Spencer addresses this by sharing, "The hardest thing to overcome was pride. I had to be willing to be completely transparent. And in order to be that transparent I had to lay aside any sense of pride and remove areas I would typically not share with someone."

The mentoring relationship is most effective in an environment that is truly open and honest, with no pretenses. Once God sends you a mentor, don't get in the way by being afraid to show weakness.

So, who is the Paul in your life? If you don't have one yet, start praying now for God to reveal someone who can help take you and your ministry to the next level.

 Jenny Funderburke is the wife of her favorite computer geek and the mama of the two cutest and craziest girls on the planet. She has served as Minister to Children at Westwood Baptist in Alabaster, Alabama for almost ten years and blogs at jennyfunderburke.com.

CHAPTER 15

BI-VOCATIONAL CHILDREN'S MINISTRY
BY LINDSEY WHITNEY

It's Monday morning and I'm navigating my car towards work. As I pass the church, I remember yesterday's children's church service. The craft was a bit too complicated and things quickly spiraled out of control as I scrambled to cut out tiny hearts for half the class. I should prep the materials better for next week, but as I think through the week's schedule, I'm at a loss to find a good time for more prep work. Between my full-time job at the daycare and commitments to family, time is running a little short. Maybe it can be done during my lunch break on Thursday?

If you're in bi-vocational ministry, you know this scenario all too well. You constantly find your time, energy and mental power being split between two major players (or more!) in your life. You might be feeling discouraged, but there is hope! You can both survive and thrive in bi-vocational ministry with a few simple procedures. In this chapter, you'll learn how to prioritize efficiently, establish goals and build a team that will keep things moving in a positive direction.

WHAT IS BI-VOCATIONAL MINISTRY, ANYWAY?

Anyone who devotes a major amount of their time to ministry work in addition to and separate from another job is involved in bi-vocational ministry. I've been the part-time Children's Ministry Director at my church for seven years. During that time, I've also worked full-time in the childcare field. I know first-hand the juggling act that accompanies bi-vocational ministry as well as the sinking feeling when another week has come and gone and goals are left unmet, again. I can recall all too well the elevated anxiety that surrounds those big ministry events as I struggled to get major tasks completed in small patches of time here and there. I bet you can relate. One way to lesson your load is through prioritization.

STEP #1: PROPER PRIORITIZATION

Ministry will never be finished. That is both good and bad. It is inspiring to know that God will always be at work, but it can also be discouraging to be faced with a to-do list that has no end. Marla Cilley, author of *Sink Reflections*, wrote, "Housework expands to fit the time available." Ministry is the same way. There is always something more to do. Limited time forces you to cut the fat in your ministry. This requires prioritization: effective prioritization.

Perhaps you were thrown into ministry and had to hit the ground running. You don't have time to prioritize; you're too busy trying to keep your head above water. Stepping back to take a big picture view of your ministry doesn't require a huge time commitment, but it is something that often falls to the bottom of the list because we simply don't know where to start.

The solution?

Take a look at the calendar and schedule a breakfast with some of your best volunteers and the leaders in your church, including your pastor. Even if you have to schedule out a month in advance, get the meeting in writing and get your friends to commit to showing up. Having a breakfast meeting with others (1) gives you a sounding board to sort through ideas and determine your true priorities and (2) holds you accountable to actually getting the job done.

At your breakfast meeting, after you have guzzled your coffee and slammed down a few of slices of bacon, open up the table to discuss the ultimate goal of the children's ministry program. Where is God leading your ministry? When kids grow up and graduate, what skills, characteristics or attitudes do you want them to carry with them?

For example, when kids leave our ministry, we want them to be able to use their Bibles and to pray with power. If we can give kids a love of God's Word and a passion for communicating with the Creator, a growing personal relationship with Him is inevitable. These are our two main priorities. Of course, every priority, program or new idea has to be filtered through our church's vision as a whole.

STEP #2: ROUTINES AND CHECKLISTS

Once you've nailed down your goals and priorities, it's time to put some systems in place so that these priorities come to fruition. Jim Wideman, in his book, *Beat the Clock*, recommends **writing down your goal in steps.** For example, if your goal is for children to be proficient in using their Bibles, your goal in steps might look like this:

- Encourage kids to bring their Bibles to church, perhaps with a special kick-off campaign

- Buy extra Bibles for kids who need them
- Write the lesson scripture passage on the board and give kids a chance to find it
- Have small group leaders help kids with their Bible during the lesson
- Have a sword drill or memory verse game at the start of each lesson
- Use your Bible as you teach, showing kids easy ways to find key books of the Bible

In our children's church, we make it a routine to practice the books of the Bible during the first few minutes of the lesson. We use a number of methods: sorting note cards, stacking cups, reciting from memory and reading from a chart, but the goal is always the same—to build a familiarity with the Bible. When kids reach the preteen group, they regularly use Bible dictionaries and concordances as they further study the pastor's sermon from the week before. There is a checklist of key Bible skills each kid should develop before entering youth group. Having this checklist gives teachers direction in their teaching and sets up a clear pathway to success. And of course, everyone loves to succeed, right?

STEP #3: CELEBRATE SUCCESS

Sometimes, in the ministry, it seems like we do the same things over and over again without any forward progress. We teach each week, we cut out tiny crosses and vacuum up glitter, but are we actually getting anything done? Are kids growing in their faith? In order to celebrate success, we first have to define it. Andy Stanley calls this process "clarifying the win." If we don't clarify the win for our ministries, each team member will be left to determine their own definition of success. As a children's ministry, we decided that our wins would be:

1. When a child brings someone new to church, whether that be a friend, parent, or relative and

2. Spiritual growth

3. Since spiritual growth is such an amorphous term, we broke it down into tangible steps—a clear path for children to travel along.

4. Knows God exists

5. Knows Bible is true (and has a message for all people)

6. Knows God made each person (for a reason)

7. Point of decision (what am I going to do with these facts?)

8. Fruits and changed attitudes (fruit of the Spirit and godly characteristics exhibited)

9. Spiritual disciplines (Bible reading, prayer, worship, giving)

Each small group leader is given a chart in order to track progress of their kids and to make notes of stories to share.

Once you've defined what a win looks like in your ministry, encourage people to share stories of success. Did a parent send you an email after they saw the lesson on kindness in action with their child? Forward that onto the team! Did a kid check out a Bible dictionary from the school library and bring it to church? Call her up front and celebrate it! If you can, set up a story sharing station in your church where people can read and write about their own God-moments. Everyone's hearts will be encouraged and your definition of success will be further solidified.

STEP #4: ELIMINATING THE EXTRAS

Once you've articulated your priorities and defined your wins, you must eliminate the extras. There are so many great programs, ideas and curricula floating around in KidMin world. If you're like me, you feel the urge to incorporate them all. After all, if it's a good idea, you should use it, right?

Wrong.

Just because it's *good* does not mean it is *good for your ministry.* You have limited time, energy and resources and you have to be ruthless in order to make sure that you are using those resources to work towards *your priorities.* Take a hard look at your ministry to see if there is some extra fluff that could be eliminated. Is there something that isn't resonating with the parents or kids? Don't think of a way to push the program more—just kick it to the curb. Save your time and energy for things that are truly in line with your vision and goals.

STEP #5: BUILDING THE TEAM

Now that you've focused in on your true priorities and have begun to put routines in place, it's time to start preparing for the future. In order to build a growing and thriving ministry, you need a team, and a good one at that. I cannot overstate what a blessing my children's ministry team is. Together, we are able to do things and impact kids for Christ in a way that would never be possible if I tried to go it alone. Of course, it will take time to build a good team, but as we know—ministry is a marathon, not a sprint. You'll get there.

The first step in building a good team is to get to know the people in your church. I am often tempted to skip adult Sunday school to take a stab at cleaning my office (hopeless), but in reality, Sunday school is a perfect opportunity to get to know people and find good volunteers. Chances are, if people are attending Sunday school, they are ready for a deeper commitment to the church, so get them plugged in.

Of course, you'll need a plan for those potential team members. Jim Wideman, in his book *Stretch*, recommends making a wish list of every single place you could use a volunteer, from small group leader to snack shopper. Create a brief job description for each potential position. When someone says, "I would like to get involved, but I'm not sure what to do," simply hand them your wish list and let them decide what fits them best. To see an example list, see *bit.ly/JiPGQ6.*

Once you've begun to build a team, be sure to appreciate the volunteers you have while continuing to look for new recruits. If you can afford it, get them team shirts to wear. Make seasonal displays on a wall or bulletin board, listing team members' names and giving a public "Thank You!" Make sure to write notes after big events and do something at Christmas time, even if it just baking cookies or sending cards.

Be sure to check in with your volunteers regularly, either by stopping by their classroom after class or periodically emailing or calling them. My favorite is a team breakfast meeting once a month to check in with one another, share stories and plan for the future. Whatever form of communication you choose, make sure it is happening *regularly and consistently*.

DON'T GIVE UP

Bi-vocational ministry can be challenging, but there are also benefits to your position. When you're in bi-vocational ministry, you can better relate to both your volunteer team and the parents in your ministry. Most of these people are working, carting their kids to activities as well as attending or serving in church. You understand the challenges that go along with this juggling act. Use this knowledge to better serve your team and the parents you encounter.

With the grace of God, proper prioritization and a good team to back you up, you'll be on your way to a thriving ministry. Keep praying and be assured that the work you are doing is making an eternal impact.

Lindsey Whitney is a Children's Ministry director at East Lake Road Alliance Church, home day care provider, and blogger at Growing Kids Ministry. Lindsey lives in Pennsylvania with her husband and two kids. She loves books, coffee and baking cookies. You can connect with her via Twitter or on Facebook.

CHAPTER 16

SOLUTIONS FOR SMALLER CHURCHES

BY **DIENNA GOSCHA**

W alking into the children's area of a mega church where I was attending a conference, I found a large castle located on the kid's stage. I learned that the castle cost $25,000 and was designed by an architect with a myriad of bells and whistles that would wow kids of all ages. As I was taking it all in, someone from my church also attending the conference came up beside me. Carol excitedly exclaimed, "They have a castle just like yours!" My castle, back at our smaller church, was made from cardboard boxes. Our resident handyman had constructed a bridge out of scrap materials, the local garden store allowed us to borrow crocodiles for the moat and a hula hoop with cheap fabric hanging from it extended from the ceiling making a gazebo. All for a cost well under $100. And yet, in Carol's mind, the castles were the same.

With creativity, smaller churches can overcome obstacles and turn them into positive opportunities. Often I hear children's pastors and leaders complain about lack of funding, low volume of volunteers, cramped space and discouragement over the number of children in their ministry. Instead of having a "we can't" attitude, start capitalizing on the unique blessings that God has given and focus on how to maximize these areas.

Within a smaller church, kids can have opportunities to learn servant hood at a young age. Put together a creative ministry team using the talents that your church has. I started with a team of three upper elementary kids, and five years later "The God Squad" had grown to 16 kids and teens. At the beginning stages, the team performed simple puppet songs; however, they quickly moved into doing backyard Bible clubs and even leading the spiritual segment of an entire week-long summer camp, engaging in drama, crafts, games, props, audio-visual and teaching. Each Sunday, The God Squad arrived to set up the kid's ministry for the church that met in a movie theater. They assisted with early childhood classes, did dramas, ran sound and PowerPoint, created props and finally cleaned up after the service. Each member of the group was assigned a role based on their own strengths and talents. With this group of dedicated kids and teens, the kid's ministry was able to run smoothly with a quality program.

Often smaller churches worry about not being able to pull off the big events such as camps, Christmas programs, VBS or outreach family events. Instead of trying to imitate other programs, capitalize on the talents in your church. Do you have artistic talent instead of musical talent? Imagine an art show displaying children's artwork, all tastefully and professionally arranged with girls dressed in black and white walking around the guests serving chocolate on golden trays while the boys usher the guests through the art displays. Imagine setting up a Bethlehem Village with biblical costumed children guiding family, friends and guests through the village showing off crafts such as pan flutes, perfume bottles, coins and weaving. Don't forget the beggar at the town well or the Roman soldiers standing at attention. Both of these ideas work well with committed artistic individuals leading the way. Imagine a fun family night Bible study where parents and kids learn together with hands-on activities such as seeing how many helium balloons it would take to lift a GI Joe or Barbie, launching an Alka seltzer rocket or working together to craft a boat out of aluminum foil. Together they decorate a family cake or make homemade ice cream in coffee cans or zipper bags. All of the activities tie to a biblical concept. Family members would not only bond with one another, but they would also have meaningful interaction with other families. Family outreach events can be effective and meaningful even in small group settings.

Instead of outreach being a Vacation Bible School at your local church, consider going to places that larger churches would not be able to go and doing events that no one else is doing. Think about doing a neighborhood Bible club, traveling to different neighborhoods in the area. Sponsor a story time in your local coffee shop where you read to preschoolers one day a week along with sharing some simple puppet skits, finger plays and hands-on activities. If you have athletes in your church, run a free one-day sports clinic or a 3-on-3 basketball tournament in your local park. Get into the community instead of waiting for kids to come to you.

Volunteer numbers can seem like an obstacle in a smaller church setting. The same people can easily be overwhelmed and overworked. Be on the lookout for those who are not engaged in ministry. Create short-term opportunities to get people excited about kid's ministry. Small drama parts, a personal story, teaching a craft or making a video are all ways to introduce people to kid's ministry. Most people are willing to invest 15 minutes of their time doing something they are comfortable with. Once they get a taste of what you are doing in kid's ministry, they may want to come back for more.

Discouragement can come from comparing attendance with other churches. Instead of making comparisons, focus on building relationships with the kids you have. There is a much greater opportunity to mentor kids and to make a lasting impact on their lives because you personally know each child in your ministry. Take time to go to ball games and school plays, send notes, shoot off simple emails, recognize birthdays and have the kids into your home. Pray personally for each child, knowing the struggles that each child may be facing. Focusing on relationships instead of numbers will keep discouragement to a minimum.

Smaller churches often will have mixed age groups of kids all in one class. Sometimes the wide age span of kids can seem like a huge obstacle. What do you do with four-year-olds in the same room as fifth graders? In these situations, older kids get an opportunity to lead and to mentor younger kids. Use older kids not only as helpers, but also to lead small groups. We learn the best when we can teach something. As the older kids teach the younger kids, they will be learning and hiding biblical truth in their hearts. Lack of funds to keep up with technology can be discouraging; however, kids still learn best with experiential learning. Create activities that will keep kids moving. Acting out stories will stay with kids longer than watching them on a big screen. Making something with their hands will help them remember a story long after they have gone home. Participating in a game show or a reality show race are all ways to help with learning retention. However, do not discount the importance of using technology today. A smaller church should make attaining technology that can complement their kid's ministry programs a priority in their goals for the future.

Max Lucado told a story about a World War 2 pilot, Bohn Fawkes, whose plane was hit by Nazi antiaircraft guns. Even though the plane's gas tank was hit, it did not explode and

Bohn was able to safely land his plane. The next day he went to the crew chief to ask for the shell that could have ended his life. He wanted it as a souvenir. He found that not one, but eleven shells had been found in the gas tanks. Incredibly, none had exploded. Later when the missiles were opened they were found to be void of explosive charge. They were empty except one. Inside, a small piece of paper was found with the message, "This is all we can do for you now." It seemed that an assembly-line worker was disarming these missiles. The worker knew he could not end the war but he could do something. It seemed so small, and yet it made all the difference.

We may feel that we aren't making the impact we should because we are in a smaller church. But the impact we make can be deeper in many ways. Never discount what God has given you to do and what He can do with it. It may seem like what you are doing is "all you can do for now," but know that it is making all the difference to the children God has placed in your life.

Dienna Goscha is Innovations Pastor at Prairie Oak Community Church in Andover, Minnesota, where she gets to daily dream and implement creative ideas. She is also the owner and author of River's Edge Curriculum, a kid's ministry resource provider. Connect with her at dienna.goscha@gmail.com or riversec.com.

CHAPTER 17

HOW TO TALK TO KIDS ABOUT THE HARD STUFF
BY BETH GUCKENBERGER

Mom," my daughter's eyes looked pleadingly into mine, "I don't understand. They seem like such a perfect family. What do you mean they won't live together as a family anymore? I didn't even know that was a possibility for families like ours."

I sighed, looking upward. I, too, was confused by the sudden announcement of some family friends to divorce. *How do I address questions I don't have answers for?*

"*Hija, lo siento ...*" I was sitting with my Mexican foster daughter stroking her back, begging God for inspiration, *what words can I come up with to ease the continual pain of rejection?*

"Dear Miss Beth," the letter started, "Our Sunday School class is praying for your family as our assigned missionary and we were wondering if you had some time to answer our questions this next month. We have collected a list and were curious of your answers. For example, are there dogs in Mexico? (*Lucky for me, they started off easy.*) Are kids in the orphanages adoptable? (*A bit more complicated, but still answerable...*) What are some reasons why people give up their children? (*Now we are getting to the tough stuff.*) There are more. Just write back. Please let us know when you are available. Love, Mr. Scott's 4th Grade Second Hour Class"

And these were just some scenarios from this week! I am sure if you work or live with children, you have your own examples of moments when storylines seemed more complicated than a child should comprehend and questions come that won't ever have easy answers. What are our choices?

EITHER ANSWER THEM OR NOT.

If you avoid the question, distract the child, or gloss over the hard truth, you have missed out on a teachable moment, a window into their heart, a heart you can shape with your worldview. But where does one start?

In my experience working with orphaned children, and as a mother to my own nine interrogators, I use the following steps to approach these tough subjects. It always feels easier to act as if I didn't hear, to redirect them to their father or to give them a pat answer or worse yet, false promise, but what an opportunity I miss when I take the easy way out. Here are some steps to the better way.

Follow this pattern, not as a rulebook, but as a guide to give you the confidence to wade into waters where you, too, might still have some lingering questions/doubts.

I. Always start with the thing you know to be true.

In my life, I have the same conversation starter whether I am talking to an orphan about the questions they have in their head (*Am I loveable? Am I loving? Am I loved?*) or I am talking to a kid eye witnessing or hearing hard things for the first time (*How could God let that happen? Could that happen to me? What should I do about it?*).

All conversations start with the truths. It's how you build the platform. So say, "What do we know to be true of God?"

He loves us.

He doesn't want one of us to be lost.

He is coming for us.

He defends His people.

He knows us.

Etc.

Start hard conversations with the construction material we know will make the house stand. Make a list of the truths you find in scripture and have them on hand, build them with the child, or offer them the truths that have been meaningful to you. Remind them of these truths in the conversations that follow. Help make truth telling their default button. When things get hard, when questions come, always start with the truths.

2. Don't shy away from the hard stuff.

Kids don't want to be coddled; they can handle far more than we think. And they will hear about the tough stuff (through social media, through school, through conversations with friends...) so it's best if they hear it from us, who can shape their worldview and speak into our responsibility to it.

And as adults, we need to understand what our responsibility is to the hard news we hear happening around the world. How should we pray? What should we give? When do we enter into the chaos around us?

It's our temptation to shield kids from hard things, to help them experience all the benefits of being one of God's kids and none of the costs, but here's the truth. Jesus invites us into His sufferings and if we are growing up the next generation of disciples, we need to teach them at an early age what it means to participate with Christ in His sufferings. That means offering ourselves (friendship, acts of service, goods) to people who might not understand our intentions. It means knowing that our teaching needs to reflect right theology. That if we are, for example, teaching about God's shelter in Psalms 91, we don't equate shelter to our nice, American homes. Our teaching should reflect God's truth and any one of His children around the world should be about to hear it and apply it. This kind of teaching, that tells the truth and not tickles our ears, will inoculate our children from the struggles some Christians experience when their shelter, as they understood it, falls.

3. When teaching about hard things, we should emphasize above all things, God's sovereignty.

When things don't go down as we wish they would, we can trust a God who never loses control. Hard news, hard images, hard realities make us doubt. (*Could that happen to me?*) Teach children upfront that above all things, God is good. Above all things, He is sovereign. Above all things, He loves us. This creates the foundation that won't crack.

We have the opportunity to teach children that hard circumstances aren't to be avoided, or suffering ignored. So many adults don't know what to do in the face of hard, so they do nothing. We not only can do something, we can be the hands and feet of a God looking to enter into the chaos of a lost world with good news! What if you role-played in your family devotions or Sunday school classrooms? Have the kids help you generate the tough stuff they see (in the world or in their neighborhood). Then act out the situation and generate conversation around how can we respond? What might each person in the story be feeling? Thinking? How can we pray? What can we do? What will it cost us? Is it worth it?

4. We can talk to kids about something in the mission community widely known as the Galatians 6 principle.

In Galatians 6:2 Paul says, "Carry each other's burdens, and in this way, you will fulfill the law of Christ." A little while later though, he says in 6:5, "each one should carry his own load." So, you might ask, *which one is it?*

In the original language, a load is referred as the weight of a soldier's backpack, about 35 pounds. Paul is telling us to carry our own backpack, something manageable. We not only need to carry our own, but we need to allow others to carry their own. To take on someone's backpack robs them of dignity and creates the victim mentality we see sometimes in social justice.

But someone's burden is our privilege to share. It's more than someone can do on their own, and helping children live out this biblical principle of carrying another's burden is an opportunity to teach a lesson that will stick with them for a lifetime.

Small children can understand what they have to offer (a smile, a seat next to them, a prayer, a toy or book, an afternoon, a listening ear, a snack, etc.). Everyone has something to offer. Helping our kids understand what it means to look outside of themselves and enter into someone else's chaos, not to carry their load, but to help ease their burden, puts our children directly in the will of God.

There is an exchange that happens when we reach out to others, and it looks best when it involves relationship. Even if the news is hard about a natural disaster somewhere around the world, or a child learns for the first time about the reality of slavery today, think to yourself as the adult in their life, *how can I turn this from a cause to a person?* Causes elicit short term reactions. We peter out over time if we work for a cause. It's hard to see progress. It doesn't hug back. But a person changes the whole dynamic. Is there someone you can introduce the child to that personalizes the storyline? Even if it's through a book or is someone they might never meet. We will sustain concern, we will sacrifice, we will pray for a person.

We can create lessons, discussion, devotionals and even crafts around this idea, but the best lesson is your life. How are you entering into someone else's chaos? How do kids see your heart break for the lost world? What things do you find yourself praying about, learning about, extending yourself for?

5. Make hard discussions a regular part of your routine.

As kids grow into adolescence, and the hard just gets harder, be the person they feel they can come and ask questions of. Open the door. Share your own questions; this is what it means to work out our faith with fear and trembling. Ask children in your classroom or in your family, what concerns them? What do they hear that they are worried about? Be intentional about a safe environment so conversation is natural. Think to yourself when you are listening how to address their unspoken concerns of *what does that mean about me? What does that mean about God? What does that mean I should do? What difference does what I do make?*

Be thoughtful about listening first, even if what they ask about hints at wrong information (think about kids who heard about the Boston Marathon bombing, or who overheard adults or siblings discussing clean water, slavery, orphan care, etc.). They might have wrong information, but don't interrupt them to correct them (and subsequently shut them down) until you are sure you know what they do.

Then start from the beginning with what we know to be true and begin the conversation of substance God is inviting you into as He molds the storyline of the children we love.

 Beth Guckenberger lives in Monterrey, Mexico where she raises a houseful of children, consumes dark chocolate and Diet Coke regularly, sleeps very little and enjoys most of all, a good conversation.

CHAPTER 18

LET THE CHILDREN COME TO ME

BY **KATIE WETHERBEE**

Often, when children's pastors want to accommodate students with special needs, their first question is, "What should I buy?" While solid curriculum, special equipment and modified materials contribute to a positive experience, the root of successful inclusion is a positive classroom culture.

Research on strong public school classroom cultures indicates that children in these classes have higher levels of achievement and better social skills. They also felt more positive about attending school. The benefits were not confined to students; teachers in these classes felt better about their teaching, offered higher-quality instruction and reported higher rates of collaboration. Most pastors would agree that high rates of learning and positive experiences for students AND volunteers would be priorities for Sunday programming. So, how can we create positive classroom cultures in church?

Fortunately, we have a model that trumps any research we can find: Jesus! He was a master teacher, and knew how to create an environment to accommodate all learners. By examining His style, and how He worked with His students, we can see how today's best practices follow His example.

He was purposeful in building an inclusive culture. During Jesus' ministry, we see several examples of His work with people who had disabilities. Inclusion was part of His plan from the beginning. Pastors and teachers who emulate this create a positive, inclusive culture in their programs. This takes careful planning, but the time spent creating such a culture is not wasted because it sets the tone for every child. Harmony Hensley, a pastor and ministry consultant for Key Ministry, observes, "Culture permeates your church and changes the worldview of those you are leading. Inclusion should be a part of a Christian lifestyle, not a lesson or series that is completed."

He knew their names. Jesus called His followers by their names, and we should follow suit! Teachers who use Responsive Classroom, an approach known for building strong classroom culture, say that greeting students by name is critical to the social success of the class. One administrator reflected, "By the end of our morning meeting, every child has heard his or her name spoken aloud. That sends a powerful message that each individual matters to the group." By training our greeters, teachers and special needs buddies to greet students by name, we emphasize their significance in the class, AND their significance to the Kingdom as well.

He knew their families. As we examine Jesus' interactions with His followers, we note several examples of "family time." Jesus took time to know and spend time with families. He understood the dynamics, and knew how to relate to them, whether at a wedding celebration or a dinner party. Similarly, effective teachers build strong relationships with their students' parents. Positive parent-teacher partnerships increase student learning, and facilitate strong and effective communication.

He stuck to a few basic rules. Rules are a necessary component of strong classroom culture. Without them, students don't know the expectations, and this can lead to a classroom that is focused more on behavior than on learning. For children with disabilities, a lack of defined expectations can also increase anxiety. Jesus knew all of this, and He created "rules" to govern behavior that ultimately led to strong relationships within his "classroom" and also strong spiritual development. Therefore, when we consider how to manage our programs, we, too, should choose three to four "rules" that will serve as a foundation for behavioral expectations. Research indicates that when children participate in developing the class rules, the social culture is more positive, with fewer behavioral issues.

He modeled how His followers should behave, and encouraged them to practice. Jesus' disciples watched Him carefully in many situations: at a wedding, at meals, and in prayer. Modeling appropriate behavior was a large part of Jesus' ministry on earth! This is also a large part of creating an inclusive culture in our children's ministries. Sheri Halagan, a National Board Certified Teacher, shared that she spends a large portion of time each school year helping her students learn how to use materials, interact with one another, and behave at school. "Kids don't know as much as we *think* they know about how to behave at school," she reflects. This is true for church classes and activities as well, especially because the environment is often quite different from that of a school. Volunteers and pastors can help to build a positive culture by modeling procedures and expectations, and allowing children to role-play and practice.

He spoke their language (and chose His words carefully). Throughout Jesus' time on earth, He modeled how to talk effectively with students. He used common language and related new concepts to familiar experiences. Many times, He spoke in short stories, and made abstract ideas more concrete. He also refrained from speaking at times. As we build our own programs, we need to recognize the importance of strong communication. When planning for children with disabilities, we need to understand how they communicate best. Visual cues, such as picture schedules and social stories, help many students understand procedures and concepts. Children who function on a more concrete level cognitively will need concepts broken down and simply stated, or even presented in an alternative format. Finally, we need to remember that our communication with the class as a whole, and with each child, sets the tone for the classroom culture. As teachers, our words matter greatly; we need to choose them carefully and use them gently.

He loved children—all of them! People with disabilities and illnesses were included in Jesus' ministry for a variety of reasons. They demonstrated faithfulness and a desire to be close to Jesus. They also helped others to understand God's sovereignty. Jesus recognized the gifts of each of His children, and He placed a high value on children's worth—not because it was a nice thing to do, but because He knew their significance: "Permit the children to come to Me; do not hinder them; for the kingdom of God belongs to such as these." (Mark 10:14 NASB)

Katie Wetherbee's writing has appeared on the MOPS International and Power of Moms blogs, as well as in Children's Ministry and K! Magazine. Katie is currently working on a book, *Every Child Welcome* (Kregel). Please visit Katie's blog, katiewetherbee.wordpress.com.

CHAPTER 19

I WANT TO BE KNOWN

BY **TINA HOUSER**

It was the second morning of VBS and I stood at the door welcoming 250 excited kids. He went through the door, not even acknowledging I was standing there, when I said, "Good morning, Justin!" His head popped up and he looked at me with questioning eyes, like it wasn't really him I had spoken to. Repeatedly, throughout the next couple of days, Justin appeared within arm's length, but not saying a word ... waiting ... waiting for me to say his name. Once I said it, he would grin and run off to rejoin his group. Finally, he asked, "How come you know my name?" I took a few moments to draw him close and share how I felt that his name was important, because he was important. His name was personal, and if we were going to be friends, I needed to know his name. I shared how I had to work at remembering the names of all the children at VBS that week, but I did it, because I wanted to. Most importantly, this gave me the opportunity to let Justin know that God KNEW him and all the other kids—by name.

Let's talk about how we connect with kids. Some of you who have worked with kids for years and years may know all of this, but we all need a refresher course now and then to point out what we've let fall by the wayside. Connecting with kids is our life calling, and we need to remember that they see their connection to God through our connection with them. *Your kids will draw conclusions about their relationship with God by the way they feel about their relationship with you.* Take your connections with kids seriously, so that none will fall through the cracks of oversight.

KNOW THE CHILD'S NAME.

Duh—of course, you know their names. But what about that first-time visitor or the kid who points you out in the grocery store? How quickly do you learn their names and would you know it if you were out of the church context? It's just about the most personal thing there is, your name. It separates you from everyone else. That's why we put nametags on—to show our identifying mark. When you learn a child's name immediately, the message you're sending that child is that they are important to you and you want to be their friend. And, if you are modeling Jesus to them, then it's easy for them to believe that "Jesus knows my name and wants to be my friend."

I'm terrible at names! So, I have to come up with all kinds of strategies that will help me. When a large event, like VBS, is coming up, I go through the registration slips and the computer entries over and over. Even though I don't have a face to go with many of those names, I want the name to be familiar to me when I do meet that child. I review whom they were invited by, so I have a reference person. And, I practically memorize who will be in each group. If all of that is done beforehand, then I can concentrate on developing relationships during the event week.

I WANT TO BE KNOWN

When first-time visitors show up, I make sure they stay with the person they came with. That's not just for their security, but it gives me a familiar face to associate them with. I also say their name as many times as I possibly can, just to hear myself say it, although it serves to bank positive reactions with the child too. A great way to make this new child feel welcome is to snap a picture of the friends together. It's a simple way of celebrating them being with you, but it's a great tool to use later in the week as you review names and faces.

Follow-up can also help you remember a new child's name. Write (in longhand—you do remember how to do that, don't you?) a postcard or note that includes their name in the greeting and also as you sign off. I know this may sound like a lot of work, but address it yourself. (I heard that moan!) There are associations you will make by writing their address. Don't disregard the importance of knowing a child's name!

KNOW ABOUT THEM.

You find out about kids by talking with them. Sounds pretty elementary, doesn't it? But, you wouldn't believe the number of times I have observed a children's class only to find the adult leaders getting to know one another and not engaging the kids in conversation. They're sharing recipes and stories from the gym, or complaining about the way a boss is treating them. There's a time for that, but it's not when you're teaching kids!

Chitchat with the kids about anything and everything. Each comment or question they raise is another reference point for you to connect to. You'll find out what they're involved in after school, how they feel about their teachers, what gets them excited, what movies they've seen, what makes them sad, how healthy their family life is and what pets have died in the past three years—all important reference points for the future of your relationship.

KNOW HOW TO CELEBRATE!

Losing a first tooth, winning a ballgame, getting a ribbon at the county fair, beating Dad at a new video game, starting kindergarten, moving on to the preteen ministry, getting a new puppy, completing a walk-a-thon, collecting cans for the food pantry ... they're all events that deserve a celebration.

We lock ourselves into a model of what celebration means by envisioning a party with friends, decorations and lots of good food. But *celebration is more than an event. It's an attitude!* There are stories upon stories in the Bible of celebrations, but those aren't the stories we normally talk about. I believe God included them in His Holy Word because He wants us to celebrate often and about everything. To a child, celebration comes in the form of a hoot and a holler, a high five, a shout out, a big smile and "I'm so proud of you." But, probably one of the best ways to celebrate with a child is to let them hear you share their reason for celebration: "Colby, did you hear that Taylor single-handedly gathered 57 pairs of shoes for our winter project? That just blows my mind!" Now, you have invited someone else to share in the celebration and you've formed a strong connection with that child.

KNOW ABOUT URGENCY.

Kids want to see your message conveyed with a sense of urgency, because that tells them that you think it's important for them to know and make their own. When you communicate the urgency of knowing Christ as your personal Savior, you've told that child that your relationship with God is so important to you that you don't want them to miss out on the best thing that could ever happen to them. Urgency speaks to the fact that I'm not going to keep anything good hidden from you—I don't want you to miss this great opportunity!

KNOW THEIR DEVELOPMENTAL STAGE.

When you ask a child to do something that is entirely age-inappropriate—either too far ahead of them or something they were doing a couple of years before—then you aren't respecting the relationship with the child. Remember, they need to be known. And, understanding their developmental stage is critical to that. What are second-graders normally able to do? Is this child ahead or behind that?

Spend some time identifying how each child takes in information—their strong multiple intelligences. Does this child thrive when visual elements are introduced? Does she clam up when we play large group games? Does this child step forward to lead when music is involved? Is he very social or does he enjoy working on things independently?

KNOW THEIR SPIRITUAL DEVELOPMENTAL STAGE.

This can be a real challenge, because the age or grade of the child is no indicator of where they are spiritually. A 5-year-old may be a vibrant follower of Christ while his 10-year-old cousin who attends the church hasn't begun that journey. When a baptism service is announced, you may have every grade level represented.

So, when teaching a class, you must be mindful of what each child understands and is committed to, no matter what their age. The goal is to challenge each child to move closer to the Lord, but in order to do that you need to understand where they are and what their next step is. In one small group, that next step can vary greatly.

A child will respect you, trust you and want a relationship with you when you show an interest in really getting to KNOW them. Can you name the kids you minister with? Can you list three things that are important to each child? Do you know something they are celebrating? Do they sense your urgency in sharing the message of Jesus Christ with them? Do you know where they are developmentally? Do you know where they are spiritually? In doing all the administrative parts of children's ministry, from organizing events to volunteer recruitment, let's not forget that it comes down to your relationship with the kids and leading them into a relationship with the One True God.

After 33 incredible years in children's ministry within the local church, Tina is now part of the KidzMatter team as Executive Editor of KidzMatter Magazine and Senior Publications Director. She thrives on being able to train those who share her passion for reaching kids for the Kingdom.

CHAPTER 20

HOW DIVORCE IMPACTS A CHILD'S RELATIONSHIP WITH GOD

BY **LINDA RANSON JACOBS**

Much of the literature and studies surrounding children of divorce focuses on emotional and social impacts of divorce. Rarely do we read anything about the spiritual development being stalled when a divorce occurs.

Often for children, the emotional and or social development gets put on hold or gets stuck in anger following the divorce. Many adult children of divorce end up walking around as adults functioning on the equivalent of an eight or nine-year-old emotional level.

For some children, cognitive development may be affected. Some children may have to repeat a grade. For the most part, children can't concentrate or focus. As time goes by, the cognitive development will begin to get on track.

SPIRITUAL DEVELOPMENT

It stands to reason if emotional, social and cognitive development can be affected by the divorce of one's parents, then spiritual development may also be hindered. Many children can't or won't trust any parent-like image. They may get angry with God asking, *Why can't you or why didn't you stop the divorce?*

What's interesting about the spiritual development though is so many children try to continue their relationship with the church right after the divorce and many try for several years. This could be because church attendance becomes a habit. It's part of the routine in a child's life. It might be that church attendance is one thing they feel they can count on to happen.

This is where we, as adults, fail the child of divorce. We don't encourage them or mentor them in their spiritual journey. Most of us in children's ministry feel the parents should be responsible for the child's spiritual development. However, when you are ministering to the child of divorce, keep in mind that many times the parents are barely functional. They may not have the ability to help the child. For the most part, children's workers don't track and follow up with a child of divorce and the child gets lost in the shuffle when changing classes or programs.

The flip side of all of this is that God's people can play a vital role in the child's life. In my own situation, we had adults who temporarily assumed the parental role with my children. These adults connected with my children and they influenced them at a time I was not capable.

The other reason children try to maintain their church attendance is they have a need to believe in God. Everything around them is crumbling and they want to believe that God is real and that He will be there for them. This is especially true for children who have attended church on a regular basis with their families before the divorce.

SPIRITUAL DEVELOPMENT FROZEN IN TIME

Several years ago found my husband and me sitting in court with a father while his soon-to-be ex-wife, the mother of his children, was being arraigned. She was in our church's DivorceCare (*www.divorcecare.org*) class, and the father had her arrested for slashing his tires.

As we spent the morning together, I asked him if he knew Jesus Christ as his Savior. He surprised me by saying, "Yes, I was saved when I was 11 years old."

I asked him several more questions to make sure he understood. I believe that he understood. But then he said something that struck a chord with me. He said, "We went to church a lot before I was saved. And then right after I got saved, my parents got a divorce. Within a year we just quit going to church. I know I should go to church now that I'm an adult and a father, but I have never developed the habit of getting up every Sunday. I work hard during the week and I sleep in on Sunday mornings."

Is this man saved? God is the only one who knows that for sure. Does he have a faith walk? I don't believe that he knows what a faith walk is. His spiritual development is locked in time. Spiritually, he is still a new Christian on an 11-year-old boy level. He only knows the Bible stories from his youth. He only knows God from the memory of his youth.

POSITIVE OUTCOMES FOR SOME CHILDREN OF DIVORCE

Some children do turn to God. They replace the earthly parent who left with the image of God taking that role. I encouraged this concept in my own family. The first Easter after the divorce, my children and I were driving into the church parking lot when we noticed a friend in the church had set up a camera and was taking pictures. As we got out of the car Rodger said, "Hey Julie and Brian, bring your mom over and let's take a family picture." My daughter screamed out, "Don't you know we don't have a family? My Dad left." And she took off running into the sanctuary.

My son was a little quieter, but his comments were just as severe. Very quietly while gritting his teeth he said, "We don't have a dad anymore. He left! We don't have a family." And he walked off with his shoulders slumped and his head down.

After church I sat the kids down and told them we still had a family. My son said, "Mom look around. In case you haven't noticed, Dad left. There is no dad in this house." I explained that we still had a family; it was just a different kind of family. I told them that God would become the other parent in our home, that He was our heavenly Father.

Today my son has a deep faith walk. God is important in his life.

WHAT HAPPENS TO THE RELATIONSHIP WITH GOD, THE HEAVENLY FATHER?

In Judith Wallerstein's "The Unexpected Legacy of Divorce the 25 Year Landmark Study,"[5] she says you will find that for the most part children's view of marriage is skewed. The ability to commit to a relationship is shaky.

With the breakdown of the family unit and the inability to understand what a marriage is all about, some of these adults will not be able to comprehend Christ's sacrifice for them.

- If they didn't experience salvation as children, it will be difficult for them to accept salvation as adults.

- If their parent left them, if their parent put their own needs over the child's, they may wonder how anyone could love them enough to lay down His life for them.

Think about this, our earthly marriages are to be a metaphor for Christ's love for His bride—the church. Marriage and fami-

---

5. Judith Wallerstein, *The Unexpected Legacy of Divorce the 25 Year Landmark Study* (Hyperion)

ly are earthly representations of God's design. God is the heavenly Father; Christ is His son. Jesus comes for his bride—the church. We can only understand this if we can think in abstract terms and understand the symbolism used in the Bible. We have to be able to comprehend and interpret scripture and the parables and accept the indwelling of the Holy Spirit. If a person is still on a child's level in their spiritual development, they will not be able to comprehend this beautiful picture.

We now have several reports and books written by adult children who experienced their parent's divorce. A very strong report is by Elizabeth Marquardt[6], a scholar with the Institute for American Values, a think tank on family issues. She also served as the director of the Children of Divorce Project. In the first part of the project, 60 interviews were conducted with adults, half of whom grew up in divorced families and half of whom grew up in intact families. This was followed up by a survey of some 1500 telephone interviews. Elizabeth has included her research in her book, *Between Two Worlds, The Inner Lives of Children of Divorce.*

Elizabeth herself is a product of a divorced family. She believes that even under the best circumstances, children will suffer emotional scars and that their relationships will suffer, including their relationship with God.

In conversations, she has relayed that one of the biggest issues she sees is the symbol of God being a Father image and trust issues, "My own parent abandoned me and now you want me to believe in God, a heavenly Father image?"

Jen Abbas is another adult who experienced her parent's divorce. Jen has written the book *Generation EX.*[7] In her book she talks about the confusion children experience with the concept of love and how a child may feel like their needs were secondary to their own parent's desires. Now when they become adults

6. Elizabeth Marquardt, *Between Two Worlds, The Inner Lives of Children of Divorce* (Crown Books).
7. Jen Abbas, *Generation EX* page 46, (Waterbrook Press)

they are told God loves them like a Father? Hmmm, how much could that be if, as a child, their needs were secondary?

When some adults hear the words, "Heavenly Father," only scenes of desertion and loss come to their minds. They don't think of God as a Father image. One lady said, "Just hearing, 'Our Father' would make a knot tighten up in my stomach."[1]

Other children feel unworthy of God's love. They feel unworthy to take their problems to such a God. They feel unlovable because they perceived that their parents didn't love them; they don't feel God can love them either.

From an 11 year old in *Growing Up Divorced*[8] by Archibald Hart we read, "I wonder if God is like my dad. Does He say He loves you and then throw you away? Does He say He will come and visit you and then never come?"

Regarding trust issues: *Is God like a Father? Because, if He is, I don't want to have anything to do with Him.*

Regarding faith issues: *I had faith that my parents would provide for me and look what happened and now you want me to have faith in "God"?*

BIBLE STORIES CAN BE MEANINGLESS

Partly because of the trust and faith issues and the unhealthy image of a parent, typical Bible stories are meaningless to some children of divorce.

Children in the Bible are left in a well, floated down a river in a basket, thrown in a lion's den and sold into slavery to pay their parents' debts. They're even left behind while the family traveled. Children of divorce worry about similar things in their everyday life. They have concerns about who is going to take care of them. Are they going to have enough to eat? Will the parent they live with leave them and desert them like the other parent who left the home? It is their perception.

---

8. Archibald Hart, *Growing Up Divorced,* page 161, (Servant Publications)

Children's church workers need to be made aware of these issues. Special attention needs to be given to the child of divorce. It may be that an adult might need to take the child aside and reassure them. Or give the child an opportunity to discuss their fears and concerns about a particular lesson.

If the child attends the church alone, chances are they will not approach the absent parent with questions or concerns about what they are learning. If teachers don't take additional time and give extra attention to these children, then they may be sending them home in a state of confusion. One also has to remember that many of these children will have parents who are not living a moral life. They come to church and we tell them to live a Christ-like life, but their parent, by their actions, may be telling them something different.

Children and church leaders can be powerful influencers when it comes to ministering to the child of divorce.

Linda Ranson Jacobs is one of the forefront leaders in the areas of children and divorce and single-parent family needs. She contributes to many blogs and periodicals, including DivorceMinistry4Kids, Relevant Children's Ministry, BiblicalParenting.org, CMConnect Radio, and K! Magazine.

CHAPTER 21
ENCOUNTERING THE BIBLICAL NARRATIVE
BY **JEREMY MAVIS**

The biblical tale, through the most rigorous economy of means, leads us again and again to ponder complexities of motive and ambiguities of character because these are essential aspects of its vision of man, created by God, enjoying or suffering all the consequences of human freedom. Almost the whole range of biblical narrative, however, embodies the basic perception that man must live before God, in the transforming medium of time, incessantly and perplexingly in relation with others; and a literary perspective on the operations of the narrative may help us more than any other to see how this perception was translated into stories that have had such a powerful, enduring hold on the imagination. (Alter, 1981, p. 22)

For me it all started with a side comment by my professor, Mark Jalovick (2000), in his Old Testament History Two class: "Children need to learn the stories of the Bible." To most this remark would have sounded obvious, and it is. Humanity's young progeny need to learn the basic content contained in scripture and, thankfully, this content is primarily narrative in nature. Stories seem to be a near universal medium to transfer both history and information. There's a reason why my own children beg my wife and me to tell them stories of when we were kids. They are fascinated by their parents' histories and they want to come to know us more deeply by our transferring that knowledge through the narrative literary device.

It's no wonder that God chose narrative, storytelling, to be the primary literary device to communicate both the knowledge of Himself as well as the account of His interaction with His people. It's been said that "the Bible is about God, continually working to fix this world through His kind of people in order to make His kind of world." If the Bible is primarily narrative and this is the literary device of choice to transmit, according to Alter (1982), "its vision of man, created by God, enjoying or suffering all the consequences of human freedom" (p. 22), then the stories are interconnected and dependent upon one another, and are not intended merely to be principalized nor disconnected from the environment in which they are found.

As a children's ministry professional, I encounter curriculum that has been organized into human constructed topics and themes with disparate Bible stories included that have been disconnected from the narrative environment in which they are found. These topics seem to be of high value to its adherents. Topics like: generosity, friendship, faith, leadership, service, attitude and prayer. Topics might even be organized in theological categories like: Who is Jesus? Who is God? Who is the Holy Spirit? What is the Bible? The standard approach seems to be: find a relevant topic, theme or characteristic that needs to be taught and engaged in with children and find Bible stories that seem to speak to those particularities. In other words, the curriculum writer or practitioner finds a problem or issue that needs to be addressed in life and looks to the Bible for the answers to that particular problem or issue.

While not an altogether bad approach to learning and engaging with the Bible (after all, at least an attempt at engaging with a Bible story has been initiated), there does seem to be one big problem with this tactic: It assumes that the Bible stories, taken out of their contextual environment, have something to say to any and every question, problem, or issue human beings have. And if I may take it a step further: It assumes that humans have even a remote idea what the main problems of life really are rather than the author of the Word. And, if you don't get too frustrated with this line of thought or hang me out to dry completely, can I take this approach to its logical conclusion? Who are we as humans to tell God what we need to know, and the Word He gave us is somehow inappropriately organized and too incongruent that we need to separate them into our own, omnipotently-devised categories?

If my previous statement causes too much consternation, I apologize. I really do. If in my attempt at pointing to a different approach causes you to shut down and not engage with a different idea then I repent. To put it simply: I merely find the, discover a relevant topic, theme, or characteristic category then go get a few Bible stories to illustrate the category in action approach, to be limiting and backwards. It is limiting because the biblical narrative is limited to the category it has been chosen to emphasize and illustrate and it is backwards because I believe that we should approach scripture on its own divinely authored terms, rather than our human devised terms.

I have been a full-time children's pastor at Hayward Wesleyan Church in Hayward, WI for over 10 years. When I arrived at the church, their Sunday school was in desperate need of some continuity. I had thought a lot about Mark Jalovick's statement, "Children need to learn the stories of the Bible," over my years of undergraduate education and I had somewhat of an untested idea that I wanted to implement at the first church's children's ministry I would pastor. My first summer I scoured the Bible and listed all the key, what I called "move the story along," stories in the chronological, biblical narrative. I then organized them into what we would locally call our "Main Street 3 year through the Bible curriculum." We spent the first year in the first five books (Torah) of the Old Testament telling the unfolding story of God creating the world and humanity who was made in God's image, humanity's fall, and God crafting a special group of people through Abraham to establish His presence in the world. The second year we continued to engage with the story of God's people in the land of Israel from the time of Joshua, to the turbulent times of the Judges and Ruth, into the establishment of the monarchy with King Saul, David and Solomon before the kingdom split in two and experienced a wild ride both in the North (Israel) and in the South (Judah) with their kings (in Samuel, Kings, and Chronicles) that eventually led to exile and a subsequent return under Ezra and Nehemiah. The third year we looked into the life of Jesus and the outworking of the church in Acts.

Each Sunday, we would quickly review the story up to the "current" point, then creatively engage with the story of the week, then offer some application ideas based on what was going on in the world and in our community at that time. The idea was to let the story be the story. Our children's ministry is organized in a large-group/small-group format, and in small groups I would often hear of the leaders engaging with the students on extremely relevant topics, themes and character issues based on the current grade and situation the students found themselves in through life.

Again, the idea was to let God show us what He wants to show us in the particular way He crafted the narrative account. To be honest, both the students and the leaders had a lot of fun with this approach because it felt more like reading and acting out *The Lord of the Rings* trilogy from week to week than simple Sunday school lessons meant to communicate a principle or truth with a Bible story attached. I remember hearing from my first grade teacher, who had taught Sunday school prior to my employment for many years, say this: "I had no idea that Moses came after Abraham. I've never read the Bible from the beginning and in order. This is fascinating to learn what God's whole deal with Abraham was and how what Moses did was an extension of the Abrahamic covenant." Yeah, she said "extension of the Abrahamic covenant"! What I was more intrigued with, and quietly appalled by, was this teacher's lack of knowledge of the entirety of the biblical story and each participant's role in the unfolding narrative. This teacher got quite an informed biblical education those first three years, and she was not in Bible College!

I am pretty passionate about starting with scripture and letting it speak for itself, but there are shortcomings that I've noticed and don't mind being honest about them. As any children's ministry practitioner could attest to, there is only so much an educator can do in an hour. If one is too ambitious, the student is on information and cognitive overload. If one is not prepared, then the students put on their own program, and it's most definitely not the kind of children's program that's cute! Communicating and engaging with the biblical narrative takes time and energy, and it often consumes much of the time. What I've noticed is that the large group time lasts about 75% of the children's ministry time and about 25% is left for small group. What seems to get sacrificed or shortchanged is the discussion and application element for more activities and kinetic games after students have been sitting for so long. The story keeps students' attention really well; however, their energy needs to be expended during the last 15 minutes or so and that tends to happen during small group.

Chronological biblical storytelling seems to be in vogue right now. I can think of several curriculum companies that have a chronological narrative program in their collection. Most of these tend to blend the two distinct approaches I've described: 1) starting with the Bible and arriving at an application, or 2) starting with a topic then going to the Bible. In my opinion, a few do a great job, while others don't. I'm not trying to knock curriculum companies or their particular products. What I do want to make sure anyone reading this understands is ALL YOU NEED IS YOUR BIBLE AND A DESIRE TO CONNECT AND SIMPLIFY THE NARRATIVE WITHIN TO AN AUDIENCE OF KIDS. You don't need a Bible College degree. You don't need any writing experience. You don't need lots of money. The last time I checked, almost every human being I know has the capacity to tell a story. And the more stories you tell, the better you get at it. My suggestion is to start at the beginning of the Bible and break the stories down into manageable segments and tell them week after week. If you are a strategic planner type, sit down with a Bible and a couple of close friends and thumb through scripture and plan out a scope and sequence through the narrative. Then week after week in your children's ministry, tell, in an engaging way, the Bible story in its chronological narrative environment. Do you need a curriculum? Not really. The really neat thing about the Internet is that if you need a craft, activity sheet or a game related to a particular story, you will be able to find it. I know because that's what we do at our church. I've bought all the craft, activity sheet and games books out there and catalogued them with our curriculum scope and sequence and then searched and catalogued those we find on the World Wide Web.

All to say, anyone can take a Bible they have in their home and begin to retell its stories in the way God has them laid out in scripture. It is simply amazing what you will discover when you encounter the biblical narrative. And you know what? When you've gone all the way through the Bible and you're done, start back at the beginning again and you'll be blown away by the things you missed the first time because you didn't know how things would work themselves out. Then when you complete it the second time, start back at the beginning again because 5–8 years will have gone by and you've got an entire new group of students who've never encountered the biblical narrative before, and you get the privilege of introducing them to God's story as it unfolds in human history. There's nothing quite like it!

Jeremy Mavis has been a youth and children's pastor at Hayward Wesleyan Church in Hayward, Wisconsin, for over 10 years. Jeremy also works for The Wesleyan Church's Children's Ministry Department and manages content for the wesleyankids.org.

CHAPTER 22

STANDING ON THE SHOULDERS OF GIANTS

BY CRAIG JOHNSON

J ason's friend was different from the other kids on the block. He rarely came out to play, and when he did, instead of joining in the basketball game, he ran in circles, jumping up and down. His parents watched, hoping their son would connect with the group, only to see that the other children really didn't understand him at all. When Jason asked his dad why his friend was so different, his father told him about autism, which makes it hard for some kids to communicate and form relationships. Jason was puzzled, and said, "I don't get it."

"Well," his dad replied, "do you ever try to talk to your friend, and he doesn't pay attention?"

"Yes," Jason said.

"Well, that's because he hasn't figured out how to communicate with you. Has he ever repeated things you were saying?"

"Yeah," Jason said, "I thought he was making fun of me."

"No, he is parroting you, trying to figure out how to talk to you."

"Is there a cure for autism?" Jason asked.

"Not yet, but I'm sure people are trying to find one."

Just then, Jason noticed that his friend's parents took their son back inside because the other kids were laughing at him. Jason decided right then to help his friend in any way that he could. "Could I find a cure, Daddy?" he said.

Surprised, his dad replied, "Well, it's like I always tell you: keep looking up, because you never know when God is going to drop something amazing in your lap."

A big smile came across Jason's face as he realized that anything is possible with God. Jason collected newspapers and aluminum cans to recycle for profit, and he set up a lemonade stand. When his friends said that he would never make enough money, he just kept looking up. With his parents' help, he planned a walkathon and went door to door asking for donations and telling others of his dream to find a cure for autism. When a door closed without a donation, he just kept looking up.

On the day of the walkathon, there were only ten people signed up to walk (and half of them were his family), but Jason walked proudly around the block, confident that he was making a difference. When a man asked him why he was looking up, Jason told him that God was going to drop something in his lap.

"Right now?" the man replied.

"I don't know," Jason said, "but you'd better duck, just in case!"

Jason called his family and neighbors and even the local news stations over to hear the announcement of the money he had raised. He was so excited that he woke up at 6:00 a.m. and checked every 15 minutes to see if people were lining up to experience the miracle. At 9:55, he ran outside to find his mom and dad, a few neighbors, some kids who wanted to see if he actually raised any money, and a local radio station that thought it would make a cute story for their lifestyles segment. Jason began to speak: "Ladies and gentleman, members of the press, thank you for coming out today to help find the cure for autism. The money we raised will help my friend be cured so that he can play basketball whenever he wants to. Let the change begin!"

At that moment, Jason unscrewed the back of his piggy bank and poured out the money he had raised during the past three months. As his mom and dad counted the money, Jason wondered why his friend with autism had not shown up. Then Jason's dad called out, "$435."

With great confidence Jason shouted, "YES! We have done it!"

In his mind, $435 was the equivalent to $4,000,000. Kids started laughing, saying, "$435 wouldn't cure a frog."

A neighbor gave him a pat on the head, saying, "You did your best son; that's all you can do."

For the first time in three months, Jason dropped his head in embarrassment.

"I did my best, Daddy," he said. "I guess it just wasn't good enough."

His father smiled and said, "Son, when you give your little, God will take care of the rest. Keep your head up; you never know when God is going to drop something amazing in your lap."

Later that day, Jason's friend and his parents returned home. Jason ran over to knock on their door and ask why they had missed the big announcement about the money he raised. The parents explained they had been visiting a developmental school that could help their son, but were discouraged because the school cost $35,936 per year. "There's no way we can afford a school like that."

Jason replied, "Guess what? I raised $435 for your son, so we only have a little over $35,000 more to go."

They thanked him, but were still discouraged, so Jason said the only thing he knew to say: "Keep your head up. You never know when God may drop something amazing in your lap."

Just then, Jason's dad came in with an envelope, which he dropped into the parents' laps. "A courier just delivered this to our house," he said. The couple opened the envelope and began to read the note.

We just heard on the radio about the little boy who wants to find a cure for his autistic friend. Our son was born with autism years ago, and at the time there was very little known about how to help him. We have always wished we could do for someone else what we couldn't do for our son. We recently sold some property, and when we heard about Jason's desire to help his friend, we knew we were meant to help in some way. Enclosed is a check for the amount we received in the sale of our property, $430,917. Thank you for letting us help your son.

The parents began to dance around with their little boy. Pulling his calculator out, the father confirmed that the check would pay for twelve years of school. No one can foresee all the obstacles he or she will face personally or in ministry. It wasn't a lack of challenges, but rather his response to them that helped Jason succeed. In other words, his response determined his experience of providence. He experienced God's best, because he saw the world from God's perspective: He kept looking up.

This story demonstrates the basic principle behind leadership: *A leader sees life on a different plane and inspires extraordinary change that helps others soar above their circumstances.* Little did I know this story would hit so close to home when my son Connor was diagnosed with autism. I remember it as clear as yesterday when my wife Samantha called me on the phone and gave me the report. As I was driving home from work, I could hear the enemy whisper thoughts in my head such as, "Your child will never be normal. He will always be deficient." I remember fighting back those voices, hitting the gas on my car, and running up the stairs to my son's bedroom, picking him up and saying, "Connor, you are more than a conqueror. You can do all things through Christ who strengthens you. You are a victor, not a victim."

When we came to Lakewood to be on staff, we thought we were coming to minister to people, but we had no idea we were coming to be ministered to. Every week after we got the diagnosis, we would hear other vertical leaders cheering us on saying, "Don't give up." "You are more than a conqueror." "You can do all things through Christ." It was those messages that kept us going in spite of the odds we were facing with our son, Connor. They weren't just my team; they were my family. When a team becomes a family, you care about people as much outside of the ministry as you do inside of the ministry. They became giants of the faith in our lives.

As we continued to walk on this journey with our son, there were times when it seemed overwhelming. There were so many questions running through our minds. What is autism? What does this mean for the future? Is there a cure? How can we help our son? There were many questions at the time but so few definitive answers.

The one thing we knew was there was no quick fix. This was a journey. We needed help. We knew God would be there. We just didn't know how and whom he would send to help us. One thing we made up our minds early on to not be was a victim. So many face living with a victim mentality when they are faced with overwhelming circumstances. I've watched others, with both compassion and frustration, accept their situation as their lot in life. I understand how we all could get there. There is nothing easy about having a child with special needs.

Yet, it was amazing to watch God bring people into our lives just when we needed it the most. Even when we didn't see a way, God used friends, family and the most special heroes of the faith to come speak into our lives right on time.

I remember shortly after the diagnosis saying to my wife that no matter what it takes we would get Connor the best help we could, not knowing at the time what that meant. We found out that most private schools for autism could run between $1500 and $5000 a month. The one we really loved was going to cost $4200 a month. I don't know about you, but even though I make a good salary, $4200 a month is a huge dent in our budget. I recall saying to my wife, "Honey, if we have to sell the house and move into an apartment, and go down to one car, we will do what it takes to help our son."

I honestly didn't know how we were going to do it. I still had two other kids besides Connor with needs. What was this going to do to them when I couldn't get my daughter dance lessons or I couldn't sign my son up for baseball because we wouldn't have the money?

Many parents with special needs kids have carried or are carrying this same burden. You want to give your child the best care, but you just don't know how you are going to carry the load. I also see so many parents without God trying to carry the world on their shoulders without the promise of anything. But God said He will never leave us or forsake us. To cast your cares on Him for He cares for you.

We had baby monitors in my son's room and our bedroom, and every night even though she didn't know I was listening, I would hear my wife praying by my son after he went to sleep, "Oh please God help our son. Don't make us sell our house. Please God help us find a way to shoulder the load." I'm listening to this in our bedroom. I'm weeping. I feel like less than a provider for my family because we have to sell our home and squeeze into an apartment. Please don't mis-understand—we were not too proud. We were more than willing to do whatever it took. It was just those feelings of inadequacy that every parent may feel when you have to do what it takes to help your family.

The day I was going to call the realtor to put our house on the market, I was feeling low. I wasn't feeling a lot of faith that day, but I wasn't feeling like a victim either. It is at these times that God will send giants of the faith like in Hebrews 11. These gi-ants come into our lives to remind us how faithful God is. He-brews 11:1–2(NCV) says, "Faith means being sure of the things we hope for and knowing something is real even if we don't see it. Faith is the reason we remember great people who lived in the past." I'll never forget one of those giants of the faith for us.

As I started to dial the realtor to ask him to put our house on the market, the phone began to ring. It was our business administrator at our church asking about Connor. I told him Connor was doing pretty good. He then said, "Craig, I just talk-ed to pastor and he said we never want you to have to worry about Conner's schooling. We are going to pay those bills and take care of Connor because we want him to be everything God wants him to be." I have to tell you—outside of my salva-tion, and my family, that was the greatest gift I have ever re-ceived in my life. We didn't have to move out of our home. It was a miracle!

When we couldn't stand on our own, God sent us people like our pastors so we could stand on their shoulders. At other times when we could only see the problems in front of us, God sent special men and women of the faith who would say, "You can make it, we're standing with you. You don't have to walk through this alone." They became giants of faith in our lives.

We are where we are today because someone encouraged us to reach higher than where we were standing. When I look back over this eight-year journey, I remember all of the giants of the faith God gave my family to stand on. I thank God for being the ultimate Giant in our life. When our shoulders aren't big enough, I remember His shoulders carry the world.

Maybe you've been on a different journey. It may not have been special needs, but it was a journey where somewhere in your life with God's help you had to overcome. One thing I've learned when going through the storms in my life is that the best way to rise above the storm is to be good to someone else while going through your storm. We could be the giants of the faith who carry kids who need our help on our shoulders, cheering on moms and dads who need our encouragement. Maybe God will use us to help someone financially or to develop programs to help those with special needs or to help those facing insurmountable odds find their purpose in life. When they have no faith, we can believe with them. When they can't see beyond their problems, we can allow God to put them on our shoulders so they can see farther than before. I would estimate less than 1% of churches in America have any program for special needs and yet there are over 30 million kids and teens with special needs just in America. Autism is now the #1 developmental disease in the world. They need us now more than ever before. We can be the giants God uses for these kids and families to stand upon.

Isaac Newton wrote, "If I have seen further it was by standing on the shoulders of giants."

 Craig Johnson is the Director of Ministries at Lakewood Church. He is the author of a new book called *Lead Vertically: Inspire People to Volunteer and Build Great Teams that Last.*

CHAPTER 23

HELPING EVERY PARENT TAKE A NEXT STEP

BY JONATHAN CLIFF

'm a father and I'm learning. I'm learning that signing my son up for baseball means I get to sit outside in the freezing cold March nights. I'm learning that my daughter will talk about her favorite songs for hours on end. I'm learning that what my kids hear at church isn't necessarily easy for them to do right away. I'm learning that my children are a much greater challenge to me than my job as a leader of children's ministries.

I'm also a pastor and I'm learning. I'm learning that setting things on fire in a building with sensitive smoke detectors is not a great idea. I'm learning that glitter is the archenemy of our custodial staff. I'm more importantly learning the best of intentions does not guarantee a real connection with my families. I'm learning that children are the most important people in the lives of their parents. I'm learning that what I teach kids at church is second in importance to what parents teach their children at home.

Behold, children are a gift of the Lord, The fruit of the womb is a reward. Like arrows in the hand of a warrior, so are the children of one's youth. (Psalms 127:3–4 NASB)

We've all been there. We start working with kids, because we love the kids. We love teaching them new things about God. We love hearing them discover new ways of understanding God's plan for their lives. Then we realize that it's much more fruitful to pour equal amounts of energy into the people these kids we love so much live with. Then we hit the proverbial family ministry wall. All that work you've been doing to connect families to your church could be for naught. And why?

*The parents aren't doing it at home. Your materials are top notch, they are shiny, and they are perfectly designed for parents ... **you think.***

I'm a pastor who works with kids and students and I've struggled with the balance of how much time to allot to ministering directly to children versus the time and energy it takes to engage parents in a truly meaningful conversation with those same children. I am becoming increasingly aware that most parents know they should be leading at home, yet don't always know where to begin. When I take the time to listen to parents, I've discovered that they are fully aware of their responsibility, but get stuck in a place of inactivity. They want to see their children succeed and grow closer to the Lord, but they want them more to avoid life's struggles and failures. They take their eyes off the goal, and begin to play it safe in their interactions with their children.

Before I formed you in the womb I knew you, and before you were born... (Jeremiah 1:5 NASB)

I think the issue is more about what we expect. Most of our materials, vision and ideology for reaching parents is created in a vacuum where every parent will do everything we create. We don't take near enough time running what we expect of parents through the filter of what is realistic. I'm not advocating lowering the standard; I'm advocating a realistic approach that helps every parent succeed at home with his or her children. The key words there were *every parent*, because most of what we create for parents has only the super, amazing, fantastical, dreamy, do-everything-we-send-home parent in mind.

There are three different ways that I've learned to keep the vision for spiritually leading families within actual reach of our parents. They are questions that guide us along the path of connecting church and family.

What could a single mother who works a full-time job do with what our church gives her? I'd go as far as to say that this single mother has the greatest parenting challenge before her. She, through whatever circumstances, is providing, nurturing and leading her children all by herself. Yet, most of what we expect parents to do at home is directing parents into something this single mother simply doesn't have the time to work into her busy day. We'd be better served to help this single mother feel comfortable doing some small steps, maybe once a week. If there is a parent who can do more, then they will naturally do more and we can reward and help them take the more ambitious steps.

Are we moving away from ideology into practicality? There are many things we give parents that cast vision (and that has its place), but do little to provide the action steps that parents so desperately need. Parents know they should be reading at home to their kids, but it's often only when schools send books home with kids that parents make the time to do it. There are tools we could put in our parents' hands that move beyond the idealistic; we just have to think more practically.

Will I do this with my own children? Conviction alert, conviction alert—this is often the step that I fail to take. I create great home-based action steps that are so difficult to find the time to make happen that I don't even do them with my own kids. I don't feel I'm being too strong when I say that it's hypocritical of me to expect others to do what I'm unwilling to do myself.

One thing we've done to stimulate parents out of this inactivity, and into achievable action steps, is to be fully present with them about everything being taught, presented or discussed in front of their children. We've pressed pause on the large task of recreating a parent education program or model, and instead looked to communicate our interest in their continuing the conversation at home. There is merit in the times of concentrated effort with parents during strategic growth times in their student's life, and we work to connect with parents in that way. However, all of the programs, models and outreaches begin with simple communication.

For you formed my inward parts; you wove me in my mother's womb. (Psalms 139:13 NASB)

It begins for us by answering the following questions: Do parents know what we are talking about? Do parents feel equipped to easily talk about what we are talking about? Is there an open door for parents to engage their students in conversation? Are we communicating to parents that we want and need their voice in the conversation?

These are just questions we process through, knowing that on their own they don't completely bridge the gap between churches and parents. Our hope is that these open doors provide the beginning of a relationship where parents trust us to always keep them in the conversation.

So how do we make it easy for the conversation to happen at home? We use everything to all communicate the same message. You've heard of them: take-home pages, Twitter updates, parent emails, Facebook stories, tattoos on the kids' foreheads, weekly texts sent directly to parents' phones, and the old standby—the weekly bulletin. All of these things, except for the forehead tattoos, are great ideas, but none of them stand on their own as great communication pieces. However, together communicating the same message, "Here is what to ask your kid today about church..." they become pillars in our efforts to open the door to parents.

Much of this is echoed by Reggie Joiner in his book *Think Orange* when he says, "As a church you establish environments or resources that serve as catalysts so the home can be re-energized as often as it needs to be. (60)" I love it when he says, "As often as it needs to be," because it clearly makes the distinction that it's different in everyone's home. That could be a home with a disabled child, or a home with children who share weekends with divorced parents or even a home where the parents are completely disengaged spiritually. We aren't called to make parents do anything, but we are called to make it as easy as possible for them to engage with us over this all-important Gospel.

Jonathan Cliff is the Director of Family Ministries at Athens Church in Athens, Georgia. His wife Starr and he have three children and have been actively involved in foster care with many other children over the years. He has lived online for six years now, writing often at jonathancliff.com.

CHAPTER 24

THE PROCRASTINATION TRAP

BY **BRIAN DOLLAR**

The ability to be spontaneous is a must in children's ministry. You never know when an illustration might go wrong or when the lead pastor might decide to throw in a couple of extra "in closing" statements. You have to be able to think on your feet and keep the kids' attention even when you weren't prepared to do so. Spontaneity is a gift, but it can also become a crutch. Sooner or later, spontaneity can become a disease that eats our best work and erodes our credibility with volunteers, parents and staff members.

As I've talked to hundreds of people involved in kids' ministries across the country, I've observed that there's an epidemic of procrastination. We excuse it in all kinds of ways, but all our reasons lead to the same result. Yes, you have to be quick and spontaneous at times, but many children's ministry leaders believe their enthusiastic personalities and the spontaneity of their ministry give them a license to walk in unprepared. They try to get by, doing the least they can do, and it shows.

How do I know this is true? I wrote a lesson about Easter and put it on our website. I hoped other children's pastors and leaders could use it. After Easter, I realized 50 had been downloaded between Good Friday and Easter—and some were downloaded as late as 10:00 on Easter morning! That doesn't even give enough time to read the lesson before presenting it to the kids. Correct me if I'm wrong, but I don't think Easter sneaks up on anybody. Every person in church leadership knows Easter Sunday is one of the two most important days in the church calendar. If it's that important, wouldn't you expect ministry leaders to make sure they're prepared?

I've heard all kinds of excuses—and I'm probably more acutely aware of them because I've used some of them myself.

- Full-time kids' pastors have told me, "My week is so full of other church assignments that I don't have time to prepare my lesson until Saturday night or Sunday morning." But I receive Twitter posts, YouTube links and Facebook updates of their status in Farmville from these same guys all week long.

- Volunteer kids' pastors have said, "I work all week, so I don't have time to prepare for Kids' Church before Saturday night." I'm in awe of the fact that they're working a full-time job and leading this ministry, but I always ask one question of them: "Did you watch any television this week?" They usually say, "Yes." Are those programs more important than the spiritual development of their kids?

- Super-spiritual leaders have confidently told me, "Brian, I don't believe in preparing ahead because that doesn't allow the Spirit to lead me." Really? So you're telling me that the God who knew everything about your kids before time began couldn't lead you to prepare ahead of time? Come on. Get real.

There's no excuse for procrastination in preparing for children's ministry. God gave us an incredible privilege and responsibility to lead kids on their spiritual journey to becoming life-long followers of Jesus Christ. Someday, we'll give an account for our motives and actions. *I don't want to stand before God on that day and tell Him, "I would've been more intentional about my ministry to Your children, God, but I had more important things to do."*

Paul wrote to the Corinthians about the day that's coming: "Therefore we also have as our ambition, whether at home or absent, to be pleasing to Him. For we must all appear before the judgment seat of Christ, so that each one may be recompensed for his deeds in the body, according to what he has done, whether good or bad" (2 Corinthians 5:9–10). There are many good and noble motivations to live for Christ, to pay attention to His purposes and to devote ourselves wholeheartedly to the work He has called us to do. We serve kids because we love God with all our hearts and He has given us a love for children. And, we work hard to prepare and serve because someday we'll give an account of our lives. On that day, we want to see Him smile and say, "Well done, good and faithful slave ..." (Matthew 25:23). That's what I want to hear. How about you?

SOME SUGGESTIONS

I know some wonderfully gifted kids' ministry leaders who create problems on their teams because they don't prepare. One volunteer told me, "When our kids' pastor went to the bathroom every Wednesday afternoon, he always came out with his message, a game and a skit idea. We had a couple of hours to pull all this together and make it work. We loved him, but he drove us crazy. We hoped he'd never go to the bathroom again!"

Create a system of preparation that works for you and your team. The goal isn't just for you to be ready, but for every person on your team to be informed, equipped, prayed up and ready to pour themselves into kids. You might try these ideas.

Make a commitment to have two weeks of content prepared. Actually, this only requires you to double up the first week, so you prepare for this week and the next week. After that, you already have the next Sunday planned, so you're working on the following week's content. This way, you'll always be prepared and relaxed, and you have plenty of time to coordinate props, games and other things with your volunteers. If you want to prepare on Saturday nights, that's fine, but you'll be working on the next week's lesson instead of the next day's lesson.

Communicate your plans and content with your team a week ahead—at least by Tuesday. You couldn't do this when you prepared the night before, but now you can. People feel loved and valued when we let them know what's going on. Send them a quick email, give them a handout or send them a smoke signal. It doesn't matter how you communicate, as long as you do it well and consistently. Your team then has time to study, think, pray and plan for the upcoming Sunday content. I've talked to lots of volunteers who love their kids' pastor, but are frustrated to death because of the lack of preparation and communication. Don't let that happen any longer. Change the culture of your team.

After being a week ahead for a couple of months, prepare two lessons in one week so you'll now be three weeks ahead. You may assume you don't need to do this, but it's amazing what happens when you let a message marinate in your mind and heart an extra week. You'll pray more effectively, think more deeply and find more creative ways to connect with volunteers and kids. Try it. You'll see.

Find a curriculum that captures hearts and communicates spiritual truth to your kids. Most of the materials on the market today are very easy to use, but many full-time kids' pastors will want to adapt content to their particular churches. Be careful: The convenience of using this curriculum isn't an excuse to wing it. Look over it two or three weeks in advance, make any changes you want to make and then give handouts to your team so they can be informed and prepared.

PREPARATION BRINGS PEACE

Procrastination produces personal and relational stress and robs us of peace. Why in the world do we put off our preparation? I procrastinated because I didn't think I needed to prepare, I didn't think my volunteers cared to be informed and to be honest, it gave me an adrenaline rush to live on the edge. And I'm not the only one.

I met Martha at a conference for kids' ministers. She has been a part-time kids' ministry pastor for five years. She loves it, but when she heard me talk about the need to prepare, she wanted to meet with me. She said, "I know what you mean about the kick you get when you have to deliver but you haven't really prepared. I'm afraid I'm an adrenaline junkie, too. I have to change or I'll lose my whole team. They're sick of me running in at the last minute and racing through instructions—only half thought through—about the activities we're doing that morning. I recently lost four of my best volunteers. They couldn't take it any longer."

I felt bad for Martha. I prayed for her to have the courage to change. I ran into her a year later at the same conference. I asked her how things were going. She beamed, "It's great! My team recently told me how much they appreciate what I'm doing now to prepare the lessons a week ahead and give them information in plenty of time. I can read between the lines, Brian. They're saying I drove them crazy before!" She sighed and looked away as she almost whispered, "Why did I wait so long?"

When I look at a lot of kids' ministry leaders at conferences, it's like looking in the mirror a few years ago. They're bright, fun, excited and gifted, but many of them are driving themselves and their teams nuts by putting off their preparations for Sunday mornings. If that's you, don't wait until your team abandons you in frustration. Do the work of ministry: prepare and communicate well.

 Brian is the founder of High Voltage Kids Ministry Resources and the kids' pastor at First Assembly of God, North Little Rock, AR. He is the author of, *I Blew It!* and blogs at briandollar.com.

CHAPTER 25

MARGIN = MINISTRY

BY **MATT NORMAN**

M argin is a term generally used when talking about money. It means having money left over after you have met all your financial obligations. While this term typically refers to money, there are other areas where this concept can apply. As ministry leaders, it is out of the margin in our lives that we do ministry. There are five areas that if you don't have margin, you will find ministry difficult, if not impossible: money, time, spirit, health and family. Without margin in these areas, you may be able to do ministry. You may even be able to do it well, for a time. But, you will not last, and your ministry will not have the same potential.

MARGIN = MINISTRY: MONEY

I was 32 years old when God called me to ministry. My wife and I had great careers and we were making GOOD money. We had new cars and a great house. The one thing we didn't have was margin. As we transitioned from career-focused to ministry-focused, we quickly found ourselves making half as much money, but not having half the bills. Living without margin was now preventing us from doing what God was calling us to.

Whether you are a volunteer, a bi-vocational ministry leader or if you do it full-time, the advantages of financial margin are obvious. This will give you the freedom to do more ministry and do it better. It will allow you to focus more mental and emotional energy on ministry and have less worry about financial matters.

MARGIN = MINISTRY: TIME

Something that ministry leaders may struggle with even more than money is having margin in our time. We often believe that if we tightly control our calendar than we are using our time well. Many of us are very good at planning every minute of every day, but this leaves you without margin. Here are some reasons why margin in your time is important:

- Sabbath: In the beginning God created everything. After six days, he rested. God is all-powerful. He didn't NEED to rest. He did it to show us the importance of margin in our time. Having margin in your time will allow you to get rest.

- Energy: If you are in ministry, I don't need to tell you that ministry is hard work. If we want to do more ministry and do it better, then we need to have margin in our time. This will allow us to have the energy we need to do the hard work of ministry.

- Emergencies: The truth of ministry is that it is not a 9–5 job. It is an available 24 hours a day, 7 days a week, at a moment's notice for whatever comes up kinda job. If you don't have margin in your time, then you may not be available at a crucial moment when a person in your church needs you.

- Creativity: Margin will give you more time to think about the things going on in your ministry. Plus with the added rest mentioned earlier, will put you in better condition to be creative with the extra time you have.

- Events: Margin can be more than simply more time in your week. You can add margin to your life by planning events further out. This will give you more time to get the right leaders involved and more time for creativity.

This is just a short list of the advantages of adding a little margin into your schedule. For many of us in ministry, this is not something that comes naturally. This is something that we would have to be VERY intentional about. It might require that we go so far as actually scheduling downtime; put events on your calendar set aside for this purpose.

I know that this may seem like much ado about nothing, but trust me—this will be worth the effort that you put into it. Do this and you will find that your work time is more productive.

MARGIN = MINISTRY: SPIRIT

In Matthew 6:33 Jesus instructs us to "Seek first His Kingdom and His righteousness and all these things will be given to you as well." Oftentimes in ministry we live our lives as if Jesus' instruction was, "Seek first your ministry and His Kingdom will be given to you." I know this sounds crazy, but this is how many of us live our lives. Our ministry becomes the most important thing in our life. Most of us do this out of a true love for God and a desire to impact the lives of people. In spite of our good motives, our actions are bad. Here are a few problems with this approach:

- When we place our ministry above God, then our ministry becomes just that, OUR ministry. It was never intended to be that way. It is God's ministry and we are simply the vessels He uses. We are the conduits through which HIS ministry flows. We are simply the ones called to translate His leadership to the people He called us to lead. When done right, it is not we who lead our ministries, but God through us.

- When God is not leading our ministry, then our ministry can only be as good as we are. I know that there are times that God has worked in/through my ministry far beyond my capacity. He did this not because of me, but in spite of me. However, when I have seen Him move the most has been when I was most tuned in to Him.

Exodus 20:3 says, "You shall have no other gods before me." Anything that we place before God can become an idol to us, even our ministry. Because we are Christians, our very lives should be an overflow of our relationship with Jesus. How much more should our ministry be an overflow of this same relationship? As such, our primary focus should be our relationship with Jesus. By "seeking first His Kingdom and His righteousness," we will find that our ministry goals become easier to achieve. We will find that our ministry is capable of going even further than we might have dreamed. We will find that the Spirit of God will work in and through our ministry to change lives.

Take a moment to evaluate your life. Is God number one?

MARGIN = MINISTRY: HEALTH

Another area where margin is needed if you are going to do ministry well is your health. There are obvious, biblical reasons for this. The Bible tells us that our body is the temple for the Holy Spirit. As such we should care for it as well as possible. Beyond the biblical/spiritual reason, I want to talk about some practical reasons.

For me this lack of margin in the area of health landed me in the hospital for a couple days. Nothing major and I am fine now. The problem is that while I lay in a hospital bed there was a little girl in my ministry whom I was scheduled to baptize. Her baptism was not about me, and one of the other pastors did the baptism for me. The point is this: because I did not take the time to properly care for my body, I missed this opportunity.

BUT, this was just one opportunity.

You see, when we fail to properly care for our bodies we WILL miss opportunities to minister. We WILL be less effective in our ministry. We WILL hinder the potential of our ministry. Now, I am not saying that our ministry depends entirely on us. I know that at the end of the day I am just a tool that God uses. BUT, I am a tool that God uses. Paul wrote, "I plant and Apollos waters, but God provides the increase." Ultimately, God is the one who causes growth, but we are the ones to plant seeds and to water. Not taking care of our health can decrease our ability to do this.

So, don't neglect your health. With the many demands of ministry, it can be easy to ignore our own needs. Take care of yourself so that you can take care of others.

MARGIN = MINISTRY: FAMILY

Sadly, this may be the biggest one that we miss. If you are married, then your first priority, after your relationship with God, should be your relationship with your spouse. Next to that should be your kids. All too often, our first priority is our ministry, leaving God, wife and kids to fight for the number two spot. Take time to be with your family. If you have to, schedule time to be with them. All around us there are examples of ministry leaders, pastors even, who let their ministry become greater in their life than their wife or kids and suffered for it.

Men, make sure your wife knows that she is second only to God in your life. Don't tell her. Live your life in such a way that she knows it. Live your life in such a way that she feels it. Ephesians 5:25 says, "Husbands, love your wives, just as Christ loved the church and gave himself up for her." Jesus sacrificed everything for the church. Likewise, as husbands we need to sacrifice for our wives. It is through your sacrifice that your wife will KNOW that she is second only to God.

Women, make sure that your husband knows that he is second only to God in your life. Ephesians 5:22 says, "Wives, submit to your husband as to the Lord." This does not mean you are his slave. It does not mean that you are somehow less than he is. But, God did call men to lead their families. Your husband cannot lead your family if you are not willing to follow him. It can be easy to become so wrapped up in your ministry that you no longer follow your husband. Your passion for your ministry can lead you to stop allowing your husband to lead your family.

Remember that God established the family many, many years before he established the church. In fact, there were thousands of years between God establishing the family with Adam and Eve and establishing the modern church on the day of Pentecost. Even as God chose to put the family in place before the church, you should ensure that you take care of your family before you take care of your ministry.

CONCLUSION

2 Timothy 4:2 says, "Preach the word; be prepared in season and out of season; correct, rebuke and encourage—with great patience and careful instruction." This is what margin is all about. Margin will allow you to "be prepared in season and out of season." A lack of margin in money can prevent you from doing things in ministry that cost you money or mean time away from work, but could greatly impact people. A lack of margin in time could prevent you from being available in a crucial moment when someone in your ministry needs you. This could be a child, a youth, a parent or a leader within your ministry. A lack of margin in spirit could find you doing ministry only from your own power. This will greatly limit the potential of the ministry you lead. A lack of margin in your health could find you physically unable to do what God has called you

to, unable to do what you love most and unable to do what you are most passionate about. A lack of margin in your family could find you with your world crashing down around you. It could find you losing both your family and your ministry. It could find you losing everything that you care most about.

Margin is not something that always comes naturally for most of us. It takes thought. It takes planning. It takes hard work. It requires self-discipline. But, the end result will be a stronger relationship with God, a stronger relationship with your family and a stronger ministry.

 Matt Norman is a Children's Pastor and is married to his high school sweet heart Kim, and they have two kids; Trey, 12 and Jayden, 5. Connect with Matt at itspastormatt.com.

CHAPTER 26

TRAINING TEENAGERS TO BE CHILDREN'S MINISTRY LEADERS

BY **STEVEN KNIGHT**

H ow can we motivate teenagers to become effective leaders in the children's ministry? This is a common question in many churches today. At first glance, this problem can look very challenging. However, there are a few important steps that you can implement into your ministry to turn your teenagers into effective leaders. Before we talk about those things, we need to start off by looking at what the Bible has to say about training our teenagers. Scripture tells us about the importance of training the youth in the church so that they can become lifetime disciples and disciplers (see 1 Tim. 4:12–13; Ps. 71:17; Prov. 22:6).

There are also very practical benefits for training teenage leaders. Children look up to the "cool teenagers," and there is great potential for discipleship between a teenager and a child. When you spend time training teenagers, you are discipling leaders who will have a powerful impact in your ministry as disciplers of children. Also, by giving teenagers leadership in the children's ministry, you are giving them a purpose and a group identity. We all identify ourselves with our family, our work, our church, etc. Teenagers will be excited to identify themselves with your children's ministry team and to have a purpose by being a leader on the ministry team.

THE PROBLEM

One common problem that many churches face is that the teenagers serving in the children's ministry simply aren't helpful. In fact, they often cause distractions every week. I've been asked many times what the key is to motivating youth to help out in the children's ministry. Here is the truth: the problem actually isn't coming from the teenagers; it's coming from us, the ministry leaders. Let me explain. Most churches bring in teenagers, ask them a few questions and ask them when they can start serving. When they begin serving, they are sometimes assigned a role, but are usually just asked to help out with things as they come up. This is where our main error is, but thankfully, there is a solution for this.

THE KEY

The key to engaging your teenage volunteers is to give them responsibility. Ask a teenager to lead a small group, teach a Bible lesson or run the video and sound equipment. The solution to developing successful teenage leaders is to give them a role, train them for the role and then give them that responsibility. Don't leave them on their own, but make sure that you give them space to lead in that leadership position. It doesn't matter if a church staff member could do the job better themselves, because the responsibility belongs to the teenage leader. My friend and colleague in children's ministry, Josh Afram, once told me that if his teenage leaders could lead in a role at 65% of the capacity that he could, he would give them the responsibility and let them lead. This not only builds confidence among your teenage leaders, but also gives them opportunities for growth. Now, before you start giving every teenager on your children's ministry team every Sunday morning responsibility that you can think of, there are a few things you will need to do before putting them in those leadership positions.

THREE CRUCIAL TRAINING STEPS

The first important training step is to get to know your potential youth leaders. Before you meet with them individually, ask them to fill out an application to serve in your ministry. This will reinforce the fact that they are signing up for a leadership role. On the application, ask for their skills and gifts, two references, their testimony, their current spiritual growth and their areas of interest for serving. By asking for these things, you can learn more about them from their written answers than you would have if you had asked these same questions in person.

Next, sit down and talk to them. Ask intentional questions to get to know them. Ask about their life. After getting to know them on a personal level, share the vision, mission and core beliefs of both your children's ministry and church. Ask what their talents and areas of interest in the ministry are. By being intentional with your questions during this first meeting, you are setting a precedent that they will be a valued part of the children's ministry team.

The second step in this training process is to help the teenager get acquainted with the ministry. Show them around, let them talk to leaders and ask questions, share a history of the ministry and give them a current ministry program schedule. Let them shadow a leader for a week or two so that they can get a full picture of the ministry. Giving them a chance to see everything will put their leadership role into perspective before they step into it.

The third step to training teenage leaders is to give them on-the-job training. Putting them in leadership roles and expecting them to lead well and grow in their skills is like explaining to a child how to ride a bike and then immediately sending them off and expecting everything to go smoothly. It rarely works. Training needs to happen before a leader starts their responsibilities, but it also needs to take place during their time on the ministry team.

The first time a teenager teaches a Bible lesson is both a nerve-racking and exciting experience. Giving them a lesson plan template, helping them prepare their lesson and checking in on them are each important parts of preparing a teenager to teach. Even after they have been teaching consistently in your children's ministry, continue to give them feedback on their lessons. When we continue to train teenage leaders, we are investing in them and setting them up for both growth and success in their leadership role.

When giving teenagers on-the-job training, get practical and personal with them. Ask how they are doing. Observe them leading in their role. Encourage them with both compliments and constructive feedback. One way to tear down a teenager is by giving them negative feedback without any positive feedback. Whenever I need to give someone constructive feedback, I follow the "sandwich model." I give positive feedback, share the constructive feedback (just one or two things) and then end with more positive feedback. It's really simple: the sandwich tastes better as a whole than it does in its individual parts (do you eat mayonnaise out of a jar? I didn't think so).

Lastly, it is important to give your teenagers opportunities to grow as leaders, with added responsibility if they continue to excel and are interested in getting more involved. Imagine having a high school student run an entire Sunday children's service! It is totally possible if you invest in your teenage leaders and build some of them up to the point that they can lead ministry teams. Giving your teenagers added responsibility after they excel in their roles might help develop them into more mature leaders who can serve in even larger capacities.

LEADERSHIP ROLES

Your teenage leaders can lead in different kinds of roles. Are you being creative with the ways that they can serve? For example, your leaders can:

- Help with set-up and take-down
- Welcome kids
- Run the sound and video booth
- Lead worship
- Act in skits
- Teach lessons
- Help with lessons
- Lead small groups
- Lead craft time
- Run game time
- ...and more!

Are you looking to incorporate specific leadership roles into your children's ministry? Here are a few more ideas for you:

- Team Leader: Leads a team of volunteers
- Bible Teacher: Teaches Bible lessons
- Visitor Captain: Connects first-time visitors with leaders
- Welcome Team Captain: Welcomes children

- Head Tech: Runs video and sound equipment
- Game Leader: Selects games that correlate to the lesson and leads them

The opportunities for leadership roles in children's ministry are abundant, so look for ways that you can give specific responsibilities to your teenage leaders.

TEAM-BUILDING

One of the best ways that you can remind your team of the goal of discipling children every week is to have a meeting before and after every program. Spend time prepping the team for the meeting and praying beforehand, then ask for feedback and pray for the children afterwards. When you do this, your team will be reminded of their responsibilities and will focus better during the ministry time.

In order to retain your leaders (regardless of their age), you have to build a team that builds friendships with one another and enjoys being together. No one wants to serve in a ministry where they don't have fun (I know I don't!). One of the best ways to do this is to hold monthly meetings where your ministry team can spend time together and have fun. Bring in food, spend time praying for one another, play some games, etc. The most important thing you can do during these times is build friendships with each of the team members. If your team has fun together and builds stronger friendships with one another, they will become more effective as a ministry team.

TEENAGE LEADER TRAINING SUCCESS

Once your teenage leaders are trained, leading in a specific role and being discipled in that role, you have achieved leader-training success. While training for your leaders never really ends, you can rest satisfied that you have built into your teenage leaders and that they can lead successfully in their ministry roles. What could have been a rowdy group of confused and unprepared teenagers has been discipled into a team of trained and skilled ministry leaders who are leading in the children's ministry every week. There will be bumps along the road, and this process could take some time, but incorporating these steps will help you reach your goal of a successful team of teenage children's ministry leaders.

 Steven Knight is an experienced children's ministry leader, speaker and author. He currently serves as a children's ministry leader at Park Community Church in Chicago. He loves to share relevant articles and ministry tools with others on his website, KidminTools.com.

CHAPTER 27

HEART VERSUS HEAD

BY **GLORIA LEE**

I n 4th grade, I auditioned for a college music professor to see if she would take me on as one of her piano students. Surprisingly, she accepted me on the spot. About a month later, she said, "for a girl who plays as well as you do, you know very little about music." At the time, I had no idea what she meant by that. That following summer, she made me take music theory classes with her college students. She also brought me in for additional sessions where I just had to listen to different pianists play the same piece, and my homework was to write what the pianists were feeling and how they were interpreting the piece. In 4th grade, I was playing Chopin, Beethoven, Bach and Mozart but I didn't even know what key I was playing in. I could read music, play well and be a pretty good pianist in town. However, if you asked me anything regarding music theory, interpretation or even if I truly loved music, I couldn't give an answer. I was completely disconnected from the pieces

I played so well. I had neither love nor appreciation for music.

That all changed thanks to my amazing piano teacher who spent more time helping me understand and appreciate each note, compilation of different notes and the story behind each piece I played. She truly helped me feel and love the pieces I played. Now, I can say with confidence that I love and appreciate classical music. I share this story because when I look at my understanding of God and the Bible as a child, it was very similar to my experience with music. I had been attending church since I was in my mother's womb. Oftentimes, I was at church more than I was at home. I was Mary in every Christmas and Easter play. I memorized many verses to win awards. I had better Sunday school attendance than school attendance. I rocked at Bible drills. I knew the answer to just about every question that was thrown at me in Sunday school. I knew a lot. I looked like the model Christian girl in the church. However, if you asked me how God was real in my life, I couldn't give an answer.

I knew factual answers, but it was evident that I didn't know how to process the facts that were given nor apply them to my personal life. By the grace of God, I made the decision to make Jesus Christ the Lord over my life pretty early on in life. However, in my mid-30s, I had an epiphany. Nobody in my life had ever asked me if I had a personal relationship with Jesus. Because I was really good at going through the motions, they all assumed that I had a thriving relationship with Jesus. This epiphany has made me super passionate about not just what but HOW we teach our kids in the church. I'm no expert in this area, but I am passionate about helping kids love and walk with Jesus.

As leaders, we need affirmation that we're on the right track. We want to know that the kids are really learning. Somewhere along the way, we thought the best way to ensure kids' spiritual growth in the church was by quantifying the lessons the kids were learning. Although most churches don't give kids standardized tests (by the way, I've known some churches that do give kids standardized written tests), we assume that as long as a child can answer the questions well and behave well, he/she must have a growing relationship with Jesus. Well, the problem with this is that kids are smart! Many have figured out how they're supposed to answer and behave to get a pat on the back!

I was leading VBS as a guest speaker at a local church's family camp. I asked the kids, "If you could ask God any question and knew that He'd give you an answer right away, what would you ask Him?" Many hands went up with answers such as "I would ask that God be pleased with our worship," "I would ask God to be glorified," and "I would ask God's name would be magnified." Wow—those are some of the godliest answers I had ever gotten. I proceeded to ask, "What does it mean for God to be pleased with our worship, be glorified, or magnified?" My question was followed by a good three minutes of silence, until a 5th grade boy shouted out "Ms. Gloria, when we give the Jesus answer, teachers don't ask us any more questions." Wow! These kids have it figured out—just give the "Jesus answer." And then you go on with life! I followed up with "Well, with me, I really want to know what you think ... and I think it's really important to understand what you're saying ... so let's talk about what it means for God to be pleased with our worship." We continued on with this conversation. After unpacking the definition of God being glorified, pleased and magnified, I asked the question again: "What would you ask God if you knew He would give you an answer right away?" Many more hands went up, but this time kids said, "Why does God allow wars?" "Why are there bad things in this world?" and "Why doesn't God just talk directly to us?" We had a wonderful time just talking about what we don't know and understand about God. I believe that our time with these kids sparked some true seeds to be planted in their hearts as they struggled with what they understand and don't understand about God.

I've come to realize that in order for kids to own their faith, they need to start thinking critically about what we teach them in the church. And for those of us who teach kids in the church, we need to go beyond teaching information. We need to ask "why" and "how" questions rather than telling them what to believe. We need to welcome their doubts, uncertainties and questions, and talk candidly about those issues. We need to take the time to sit with the kids and unravel why kids say what they say. Rather than being quick to correct their misunderstandings, we need to help kids sort through their understandings.

So what does this all look like? I don't have all the answers, but the following are some things we have started doing in our children's ministry:

We set aside time for kids to respond every week in small groups. When we talk about hope, we ask kids how they have experienced hope in their personal lives. And if they haven't experienced hope, what they hope for. Sure, we get answers like "I hope for a Star Wars Lego set." But we also get answers such as "God gave me hope to feel less lonely when I didn't have friends at school." We meet the kids where they are, and sometimes we get blank stares too. This is challenging for some of our leaders, but I tell them not to prompt answers from the kids; rather, let them come up with their own thoughts even if it's silly or non-sense, and meet them where they are—and keep asking questions to probe and understand their thoughts. This is where we really get to know where their hearts are. We don't want them to just regurgitate answers we give them, but we want to know where they really are so we can start there. Spiritual formation isn't linear, and we can't treat all kids the same way.

We still encourage kids to memorize verses, but we put just as heavy importance on understanding the verse, if not more. We take the time to help kids unpack the meaning of the verse in their own words. Each week after we memorize our verse, we go through each section of the verse to make sure it makes sense to the kids in their own lives.

We have stopped focusing on disciplining bad behavior, but started focusing on dialogging with kids and parents about why they're having a bad day. Kids are entitled to bad days—adults have them all the time. The difference is, adults know how to hide our bad moods better than kids (most of the time). When kids misbehave, we ask them if something happened that morning or week that caused them to have a bad day. We let them know it's okay to have bad days; it's just part of life! We dialogue about what happened, how we can help the situation and we pray together. If it's persistent behavior, we dig into what's happening in this child's life. We journey with the parents so we get to the whys of the child's behavior. Through this process, we weave in God's purpose and desire for our lives. We talk about what God might be teaching us through tough times. We make sure kids understand that following Christ doesn't mean life is easy and perfect, but we handle problems in life differently.

We regularly talk about God Sightings—where we see God active in our lives! We leave nothing to coincidence, but acknowledge God's active presence in our daily lives. We do our best to weave God into the reality of our lives, even in bad times. God isn't reserved just for Bible lessons, but we see God in all aspects of our lives, even when we're not at church!

We welcome all thoughts and answers. In fact, I often start out by saying "Lots of times, we want to answer go to church, read the Bible, pray and trust Jesus. I've already said it, so you tell me some other thoughts you have!" And I refrain from saying, "That's not what I was looking for" or "Can you share something else?" no matter how nonsensical they sound. I simply say, "Thanks for sharing your answer" to just about every thought that is shared. I want the kids to know they're in a safe place where they can openly share their thoughts—and when we hear something alarming, we follow up to better understand where they're coming from.

I will be honest. This hasn't always been easy. In fact, it was much easier to teach the lesson and review how much they remember the lesson the following week. However, investing in kids to help them process and understand what God is up to has been much more rewarding, not to mention the relationships that have come out of it! Recently, I received an email from a child who was in my very first ministry. She is now in her late 20s, and she wrote: "I can tell you that growing up in a Christian family where the parents are active in the church does not guarantee that the child feels loved at home. I was a child desperately craving for love and attention. All of my problems as a child almost felt like they disappeared when I felt the embrace and love of the teachers (at church). And the fact that I was able to be silly around them meant I felt safe enough to be myself."

Just as I eventually gained true love and appreciation for the music that I had played so well as a child, my prayer is that every child would grow in love for God and experience His goodness daily. I was a child who grew up with a lot of knowledge about God, and while that may not have been entirely bad, I have cousins who have the same knowledge without having a relationship with Jesus. I pray for each child to have deep love for Jesus that moves them to obedience.

Gloria Lee is pastor of children and families at the Jefferson campus of Young Nak Celebration Church in Los Angeles. Connect with her at gloriaslee.wordpress.com.

CHAPTER 28

IT'S ABOUT THEM, NOT YOU

BY **MELISSA MACDONALD**

As a KidMin coach and consultant, I spend much of my time meeting with leaders in children's ministry. Everywhere I go I find that leaders are frustrated, angry, hurt, baffled, tired and giving up, because they simply can't find volunteers to do the best ministry in the church. (Whoops, did I just let a little bias show through?)

I firmly believe and teach that *recruiting volunteers has a whole lot more to do with what God wants to do in the life of the volunteer than it has to do with filling the holes in a kids' ministry.* When you approach recruiting from that angle, your entire focus shifts. You no longer recruit for holes, but you recruit for possibilities. An effective leader cares about people over the program.

Your ministry is not yours—it is God's. He has amazing plans, not only for the program and the kids, but also for you and your volunteers. Recruit as a leader. Look for people with gifts and abilities, and don't be afraid to speak truth into their lives. Do it with integrity and conviction, but step out and speak. Remember, you are recruiting for the person, not the program.

JIM'S STORY

There was something about him, a quality that was worth noticing. Jim was a part-time farmer and a full-time tax accountant. In charge of revamping the children's ministry, I had my eye on Jim. He was great with adults, but when he was with kids, he was amazing. Nondescript and a little nerdy, Jim had no outward "coolness" and yet kids flocked to him. He also noticed the kids who didn't notice him—the ones who stayed away from the group, the ones who were obviously hurting or angry, the ones who could so easily get lost in the shuffle. Jim, in his shirt and tie, plopped himself down by these kids to make connections with them. Other adults watched him and followed suit.

I invited Jim to be a part of our midweek planning team and he reluctantly agreed, saying he was quite sure he didn't have much to offer. In our first meeting, I openly approached Jim about leading our small group leaders. He was taken aback and rendered speechless. When he got over his shock, he sputtered disbelief and assured me that he wouldn't be any good at that.

I was recruiting Jim for his obvious gifts, but he had not yet seen those God-given gifts in himself. I knew I was being called to speak truth into his life. I specifically pointed out his obvious gifts. I told him I believed he was a leader of both adults and children, and I firmly stated I believed he was more than equipped to do this. Not only was the Holy Spirit obviously present but my entire team was nodding along with me and muttering "uh-huh." As I spoke truth, it was as if Jim cracked open and for the first time began to believe there might be a place for him. Jim agreed to pray about it and I'm pleased to say that today he is a gifted leader of our small group leaders. He needed help for about a week and now he meets with his team, gives them ideas and prays with them. He is a completely different man.

I recruited Jim for Jim and not to fill a hole. I knew without a shadow of a doubt that God was going to do something in Jim as a result of him working in our kids' ministry. That night was a defining moment in his life.

Too often, we have the wrong mindset when we recruit people to children's ministry. There is no doubt that children's ministry requires the largest amount of volunteer force of any ministry in the church in order to make it happen. Holes, desperation and even panic can seem inevitable at times. However, when your focus changes and you approach recruiting from a true ministry perspective, lives can be changed.

When you approach recruiting as a leader, instead of a manager, you allow God room to change lives. Be obedient in that, and God will fill each of your holes with abundance.

THE SHIFT

Keeping in mind it's about people over programs, a shift in focus must happen in how you recruit. We cannot expect people who walk in the door of the church, sit in the service, and walk back out the door to develop a passion for children's ministry. If God is at work in your ministry, share it! I find myself frustrated because 99 percent of the time, the people who complain to me that their congregation or leadership doesn't seem to care about children's ministry are not doing a thing to promote and share what God is doing in their ministry. Children's ministry is the best place to serve in the church! Unconditional love, hilarious stories, honesty, hugs, conversions, life impact and more ... it all happens in kids' ministry. Why wouldn't somebody want to get involved?

Your focus is people and it is innate within people to desire to be a part of something big, something great. Create a buzz. Start sharing what's going on in your ministry. As people see that God is at work in the world of children's ministry, they are going to want to get involved.

In my days as a children's pastor, I was intentional about sharing with the congregation and leadership what was happening in our children's ministry. After a 5th and 6th grade retreat, I followed up with a 2-minute video and a celebration for the 11 kids who accepted Christ. After a great time at a children's ministry conference, I personally emailed our elders and leaders and gave them specifics on what I had learned and I thanked them for investing in me. After a VBS with record-breaking attendance, I posted stats and snippets of stories on our church Facebook page. My church and leadership were aware of what was going on in our children's ministry and they wanted to be on board.

Mark and his wife, Faith, were drawn to our kids' ministry because it seemed like we had so much fun. We had successfully created a buzz and they wanted to be a part of it. They weren't very deep spiritually, but I could see potential in them; it was about them and not just the program. I asked them to join our FX (family experience) team in the role of stage manager and co-host. They were naturals. As our team met monthly, Mark and Faith began to grow. The potential I had seen blossomed into gifts and abilities far beyond what I could ever have imagined. As they grew in their roles, they grew in their relationships with Jesus. Soon they were regular Sunday school teachers and Mark was one of my best summer camp counselors. We created a buzz, it attracted people, we recruited them and they grew. *It was more about what God wanted to do in them than what God wanted to do in our children's ministry.*

G'S STORY

Recently, I received a one-page handwritten letter from an Army base in South Carolina. Twenty-year-old G had written to tell me what God was doing in his life. "It's not camp, Miss Mel, but I'm having a great time and God has been shaking and breaking me down, lifting me up and teaching me lesson after lesson." I cried tears of joy over receiving such a special letter.

Six years ago, I took G on as a CIT (counselor in training) for the cabin of boys we were taking to camp. It was a risk, because G was a long shot. You know the kind I mean. He didn't wear a belt with his too-big pants, he had just enough crazy in him to be scary, he wore a poncho regardless of the weather and he danced to the beat of his own drum. Yet there was a quality about him that could not be denied. I also knew with every fiber of my being that God wanted to work in his life. I partnered him with a strong male head counselor, had a "come to Jesus" talk with him and kept a close eye on him. God took the iffy and the messy and made something remarkable out of G. He was a natural born leader with a heart for kids and Jesus. At camp, in a safe environment, he was given the opportunity to grow and mature. I took him back three years in a row and together we worked together to fine-tune his natural leadership tendencies. Last year I was privileged to return to speak at the same camp I used to direct. After an absence of two years, I walked onto the grounds and one of the first people to greet me was G. With tears in his eyes, he hollered "Miss Mel!" and gave me a crushing bear hug. It was his turn to be a head counselor and have a messy CIT of his own. The cycle continues all because a person, not a position, was recruited and God was allowed to do the work He wanted to do.

Leaders in children's ministry, your focus has to shift! Whether your title has the word "pastor" in it or not matters little. You are called to lead people. You are called to shepherd. You are called to be a part of life change. Do not get so caught up in thinking that life change has to happen in kids that you forget about the adults involved in your ministry. Shift your focus to people over programs, share what God is doing in your ministry and recruit with new eyes and a new heart.

 Melissa MacDonald currently serves as the National Children's Ministry Consultant for the Christian and Missionary Alliance, as well as doing independent consulting and coaching. Connect with her at melissajmacdonald.com.

CHAPTER 29

I WANNA BE LIKE YOU

BY **TINA HOUSER**

I am the obnoxiously proud grandma to 3-year-old twins, Bowen and Kendall. Although I've been doing children's ministry for more than three decades, they are giving me a refresher course in early childhood development. I actually have a computer file called "Observations of B & K." It's amazing the little things you're reminded of—things that you know, but have somehow gotten filed back in the dark places of your grey matter. One of those things I've been reminded of this past year is that kids are great imitators! They live to imitate! They are watching your every move.

I was zipping from store to store doing errands before heading out of town. There were so many little things that went through my head that I wanted to remember, but nothing to write them on in the car. I did have a pen, though. And, I did have the palm of my hand. At each stoplight, I grabbed the pen and scribbled a note on my hand (otherwise known as a palm-pilot). Before heading back home, I dropped past to give hugs and kisses to the twins. Kendall and I played for a few minutes as she gave me an imaginary manicure. She turned my hand over ... and GASP! Her eyes opened wide as she took in all the marks on my hand. "Mawmaw, what's dis?" There it was. All the pen marks noting precious details for me to remember. "Oh, Kendall, Grandma was bad. She wrote on her hand. We should never do that." As I rushed to scrub the marks from my hand, I quickly jotted down what I needed to remember, but this time on paper. I knew this was not the end of the story. A few weeks later I received a phone call that I thought was from my daughter-in-law. It wasn't. It was from Kendall. On the other end I heard, "Mawmaw, I in twubble" to which I replied, "What's the matter, Kendall?" She said, "I wote on my hand. You in twubble, too!"

Children learn everything through imitation. They learn physical things like: toilet training, how to hold a spoon, how to drink from a cup, how to throw a ball, how to do a somersault. They also learn gestures and expressions. Sometimes it may feel like the child is the adult's mirror, because a tongue stuck out, a hand raised, or the way feet are crossed on the coffee table are mimicked to the last detail. They imitate phrases and reactions. If you listen to children as they play, you will often hear a phrase that one of their parents uses frequently. And, they will also imitate reactions to joyful and challenging experiences, sometimes posing some rather embarrassing situations. Children's brains have not developed the filters that block out their impressions, so everything is fair game.

Just as kids mimic actions, they will also mimic attitudes and beliefs of those they spend the most time with. That puts a lot of responsibility on each significant adult in a child's life to say and do only what they want imitated. Children imitate their parents; they reflect their parents. So, who should these significant adults be imitating and reflecting in order to make sure kids are getting it right? Just as a child imitates a parent, so we should be imitating our Heavenly Parent. Philippians 4:8–9 gives us guidelines that are well worth imitating:

> *Finally, brethren, whatever is true, whatever is honorable, whatever is right, whatever is pure, whatever is lovely, whatever is of good repute, if there is any excellence and if anything worthy of praise, dwell on these things. The things you have learned and received and heard and seen in me, practice these things, and the God of peace will be with you.*

Here are a few questions to answer that will help you start evaluating what you want the kids in your sphere of influence to imitate.

DO I VERBALIZE AND DEMONSTRATE MY GRATITUDE?

If you're grateful for something, you need to express it. We can drill kids over and over again by saying, "What do you say?" when we're trying to get them to say thank you, or we can live such lives of gratitude that all they know is to imitate it. Since Bowen and Kendall were old enough to put words together, they have always spontaneously interrupted every family meal to say, "Thank you for making this good food," "I like this food a lot" or something to express their gratitude. Never were they told to do that. Never. They were imitating their father, who learned because he imitated his father. A meal has never been placed before my husband and son when they didn't thank me for preparing it. Gratitude should seep out as you deal with people, in big and small ways. "Thank you" should flow from your mouth freely and abundantly. Sometimes, the situation feels like it deserves more than words of gratitude, so let kids see other physical ways gratitude can be expressed.

WHEN DO I PRAY?

Is every personal conversation you have with God done in private? How can children imitate how you pray if they never watch and listen? Help children realize they can talk with the One who created them at any time of day, in any situation. When someone gets a scraped knee, don't just grab a bandage. Say, "Dear God, Millie just hurt her knee. Please help it to stop hurting." When you're playing with bubbles on a beautiful day, say, "Thank you, Lord, for this day and for these silly bubbles!" When everything you do and say is in God's hands, and you acknowledge that through talking with Him—out loud—throughout the daily routine, children will imitate that freedom of going to the Lord anytime, anywhere. Wouldn't it be nice to instill a dependence on prayer in them when they're young? We can when we allow them to imitate that kind of prayer life.

HOW DO I LIVE OUT SERVING OTHERS?

Talk about the conditions in this world that break your heart, because they break the heart of God, but talk alone won't make kids servants. There's nothing there to imitate except the words. They need to see what you do in reaction to the things that break God's heart. Take kids along when you deliver food to the poor and help them understand that you help these people because it makes God happy for us to care about others. Become more spontaneous in responding to a need, even a small need, like someone needing a door opened or a diaper bag carried. Don't wait for those opportunities to be organized and right at your fingertips, but make an extra effort (hurry across a room or leave what you're doing) to help someone. Matthew 5:16 reminds us to, *"Let your light shine before men in such a way that they may see your good works, and glorify your Father who is in heaven."* Kids will see your good works. They will glorify the Father and begin imitating you by doing likewise.

IS SCRIPTURE MEMORIZATION IMPORTANT TO YOU?

Are you regularly hiding God's Word in your mind and heart? If it's important to you, it will be important to kids. Too often we think that scripture memorization is something for kids and our brains are too old to be able to do that. It's not just for kids! You're never too old, and the impact on kids is phenomenal! When they hear you referring to scripture easily because it's in your long-term memory, they sense that it's important in the daily routine of your life. When you pray scripture and call on the promises of God, kids want to do what "big people do," and if this is part of what "big people do," then they'll want to do it, also.

What other questions can you ask that will help you realize what kids are imitating?

- How quickly do I apologize or offer forgiveness?
- Am I judgmental?
- Do I show respect?
- How do I talk about people when they're not around?
- How do I handle frustration?
- Do I tell the truth in all things?

There's a recent commercial of a little boy following his father around the house, doing everything exactly as dad. The father slouches on the sofa with a pop, and the son does likewise with his pop. Mom wants her son to drink more water, so she grabs not one, but two bottles of water. She hands one to her husband, and the boy naturally reaches for his, substituting the pop that each of them had for a bottle of water. The boy was totally happy with the pop being taken away. Why? Because he was imitating his father. There is great potential in tapping into the power of imitating.

With confidence, and I have to believe some hesitation, because he knew the enormity of what he was saying, Paul writes in 1 Corinthians 11:1 to, *"Be imitators of me, just as I also am of Christ."* Be aware that there are always little eyes watching you, anxious to imitate every word, action, and attitude that you let them hear and see. Live with confidence and a healthy hesitation of the huge responsibility it carries.

After 33 incredible years in children's ministry within the local church, Tina Houser is now part of the KidzMatter team as Executive Editor of KidzMatter Magazine and Senior Publications Director. She thrives on being able to train those who share her passion for reaching kids for the Kingdom.

CHAPTER 30
SUCCESSION: WHO'S NEXT?
BY **RICARDO MILLER**

O ne of the biggest mistakes I made when I started out in children's ministry leadership almost two decades ago was not leading with this thought in mind: Who's next? What am I leaving as a model to the next children's ministry leader to follow? Someone will be in this position after me; have I prepared and set the stage for them to lead well? These are vital questions that should be asked as you enter your position of leadership.

Unfortunately many children's ministry leaders don't ask the hard questions and go on to operate the same way, running a one-man show. Much like I did in my young, zealous days. Yes, experience is the best teacher. It would be much more rewarding if we allowed the experiences of others to teach us the lessons best suited for our development and growth. The highest manifestation of true leadership is to identify one's replacement and to begin mentoring him or her.

When I started in ministry in 1995, I was very passionate about the call of God to reach children. I volunteered at an orphanage in the Bahamas and it was through that experience that I formed my first organization, Words at Work Children's Ministry. I began meeting on Saturdays and Sundays with kids, giving my time, my talent and my treasure, often my entire paycheck, to the work of the ministry. While my efforts were very noble (they truly came from the heart), my efforts were not grounded in wisdom. Through my passion and heart to want to make a difference in the lives of young people, I began to develop my leadership skills and went on to open kids clubs in public schools. The movement picked up momentum very quickly. Soon it began to multiply at such a rate that we grew to hosting twelve clubs in a span of just a few years with over 1,200 kids in the public school system.

By the year 1999, I was awarded "The Most Distinguished Youth Leader" and the organization was recognized as the "Fastest Growing Youth Organization" by the government of the Bahamas. How amazing does that sound? Sounds like we were making waves. Yes it does. Sounds like we were doing big things. Yes. We were. Sounds like we were going places. Yes. We ... the only problem is there was no "We." It was in large part "Me." I was not completely alone, but there is a stark difference between executing tasks related to making things happen in an organization and allowing others to take ownership of that responsibility, and then empower them to train someone else for when the time of transition comes.

During that time, I'd also become politically involved with the youth arm of the Bahamas government. To say it mildly, I had my hands full. This was without a full staff, without a solid volunteer base. This was often without solid, consistent funding. My vision was big. My passion was BIGGER.

How many positional leaders lead the same way as I did before I allowed experience to teach me some very valuable lessons that I will share in this chapter? In this instance I use "leaders" loosely and preface it with positional. Being in front doesn't make one a leader. He who calls himself a leader and has no one following has mistaken his position.

Plan your departure the day you begin. Develop a team of individuals around you who can be trained to carry the mantle when your season shifts. You are dispensable, mortal and temporary. Start with the attitude, "My greatest job is to leave someone greater than myself in this position." You start planning immediately to leave this position. The secret to succession begins with the leader's acceptance of his mortality. It begins with a consciousness ..."I am temporary" ... that allows confident leaders to begin planning their departure. Who knows how long your tenure will be? They key is being so comfortable and confident with your position that you are willing to let someone in.

Great children's ministry leaders must:

- Find the courage to mentor—you aren't effectively leading if there is no one following you. Jesus chose twelve disciples who would effect change in an entire world.

- Secure a legacy for the next generation.

- Transfer their deposit to the next generation.

- Measure success by the success of their successors.

Ministry is generational. This principle is important for all leaders to understand and should become the foundation of the leader's obligation to prepare the future leaders. If you aren't preparing for transition, you have to ask yourself, who will carry on in my absence? Will the work you put in to build the ministry be carried on or will it fall apart when you are no longer there?

The Gospel is never given for one generation, but is transferred as a trust to the leadership of the day. True vision is dynamic, fluid and flexible. Every generation of children's ministry leaders owes the debt of vision to the next generation. Ignoring this principle has been the source of great failure for leaders throughout history.

The last thing any of us wants is to be replaced. We want to protect our position, and none of us wants to feel we are not significant. Yet true leaders seek to replace themselves. Successful succession requires working yourself out of a job and making room for the next phase of leadership. It's important for you to always THINK NEXT. Jesus Christ addressed this with His disciples:

John 16:7 "But I tell you the truth: It is for your good that I am going away. Unless I go away, the Counselor will not come to you; but if I go, I will send him to you."

All leaders should have this attitude. In other words, "It is expedient that I go away. It is necessary that I leave you. It is in your best interest that I vacate this position."

The measures of great children's ministry leadership are not how well we maintain followers but how well we:

- Produce leaders.
- Judge success by the diminishing dependency of the followers.
- Make ourselves increasingly unnecessary.
- Prove we are able to leave.
- Produce replacements who can lead others in our department.

All leaders should strive to execute their duties, reach milestones, achieve major progress and fulfill the vision for their department. However, they also should work to produce the next generation of leaders who will value, protect, preserve and build on those achievements.

When I got married and moved to Texas, everything in my children's ministry in the Bahamas stopped. Oh boy. All of the kids clubs and activities going on a weekly basis for hundreds of kids came to an abrupt halt because succession was not a thought at the time. On paper, our organizational structure looked great, but in reality it was not executed the way it was written. As I led the children's ministry at my home church back in the Bahamas and pioneered the fast growing kids programs through Words at Work Children's Ministry, the idea of succession was not even considered because we were making waves and doing big things, but unfortunately we were only operating in the NOW instead of THINKING NEXT.

After my early experience as a children's ministry leader, I came to appreciate the idea of not only building a great kids ministry that children will enjoy now, but of creating a structure to ensure what is being built can be passed on to other men and women who have a passion and commitment to reaching children.

Too many times I have seen great works, sacrifice and hard-fought victories squandered and devalued by the irresponsible, insensitive, abusive acts of a succeeding generation of leaders who have little or no appreciation for the blood, sweat and tears expended by those of the former generation.

The most important responsibility of leadership is to prepare for succession. The most valuable goal of leadership is not to succeed in the present, but to secure in the future. You are only truly successful in leadership if your accomplishments and achievements are preserved and perpetuated for posterity. As children's ministry leaders, it is not what we achieve that counts. It is what we transfer.

Building people to protect and preserve our department is more important than building departments. Leading beyond your season is the ultimate accomplishment of true leadership. It takes a lifetime to accumulate the knowledge, wisdom, skills, insights and experience that make you an outstanding children's ministry leader. It would be a tragedy to see the wealth of that life-deposit go to waste.

Experience is not just the best teacher, it is the only teacher—whether it's your experience or someone else's.

Winston Churchill wisely observed, "The farther back you can look, the farther forward you are likely to see." So when you and I gaze in the rearview mirror at people who have already been there and done that, it gives you the advantage of tremendous help and guidance.

What the Apostle Paul shared with young Timothy is a clear directive for us as children's ministry leaders: "And the things that you have heard from me among many witness, commit these to faithful men who will be able to teach others also" (2 Timothy 2:2).

So whatever knowledge, wisdom or experience you receive in life, take it, run with it and think SUCCESSION ... WHO'S NEXT.

- Learn the way!
- Go the way!
- Show the way!

HOW I LEARNED MY LESSON

After operating my children's ministry in the Bahamas for almost five years, from 1995–2000, I met my lovely bride Isha. She came alongside to help, but due to my hectic schedule and numerous commitments, I was wisely advised by my pastor to relocate from the Bahamas to my wife's home area in Texas. We could start over and build the organization with structure that would sustain it for the long term. I would ultimately go on to serve as children's pastor at a local church in the Dallas area where I've been able to put in place key leadership principles that will allow anyone to lead the department well.

In my 18 years in children's ministry, I have met dozens of individuals who were blessed with great experiences and have achieved outstanding success in children's ministry. Unfortunately, only a select few have intentionally chosen to invest the knowledge they have acquired into the lives of others.

For whatever reason, far too many choose to keep what they have learned to themselves and, as a result, deprive upcoming potential children's ministry leaders of the necessary skills and wisdom they have learned over the years. Let's remember in our pursuit. Ministry is really a generational relay with each succeeding generation responsible for passing the baton safely to the next with all the distilled knowledge, experience and wisdom intact.

Ricardo Miller is the President/Founder of Ricardo Miller Children's Ministries ad serves as the Student Ministry Pastor, overseeing ages birth through 18, at Pathway of Life Church in Dallas, Texas, where he lives. He is the host of the "Children's Ministry Today" Radio Show.

CHAPTER 31
LEADING VOLUNTEERS
BY **GLORIA LEE**

A s I enter my 20th year in children's ministry, I'm convinced that being a good minister to children requires investing my time, energy and resources in children's ministry staff and volunteers. One of the biggest myths about children's pastors/directors is that we spend all our time teaching children, and that's it! The truth is I've spent less time interacting with kids during the time I've been a children's pastor than when I was a volunteer. I may interact with lots of kids at once, but I don't get as much one-on-one time to really get to know an individual child or family. Children's ministry just can't run effectively without quality volunteers who personally invest into the lives of an individual child and his/her family. It's impossible for me to know every child in our ministry well. The last time I knew every child and family in our ministry, we had 20 kids as a brand new ministry. But as our ministry grew, the volunteers were the ones who got to know the kids in their small groups more intimately, as well as their parents and the stories of each child. I come into the picture when there are specific needs, but I still don't know all the names and faces of the 100 kids who come into our ministry week after week.

Most of us only have one to two hours per week with the children who walk into our church. Thus, it's crucial that we make that short time count because we have the unique opportunity to make eternal impact in the lives of kids by partnering with their parents. Because we're passionate about reaching every child, the more kids, the more volunteers we need. In our church, each small group leader has four to eight children under their care throughout the year. I make it a point to impress upon the volunteers that it is their job to connect with each child in their small groups each week. It is very important to us that each child is greeted, talked to about their past week, asked about the week's lesson for understanding and application, prayed for and hugged. I can't do this for 100 children, but the volunteers can do this for their four to eight children in their small groups! Therefore, I make it a priority to develop, equip and lead volunteers to be crucial parts of the team! Once again, I repeat: children's ministry can't run effectively without quality volunteers who personally invest in these kids!

So how do I invest in my staff and volunteers? Below are some practical practices that I have learned over the years that have helped me lead volunteers.

My general rule of thumb is—what I want the kids to receive from the volunteers, I provide that same care to the volunteers. We hear too often of volunteers who burn out because they've been giving and giving without being cared for. I try my best to connect with each volunteer. We have a team huddle each morning before we start our ministry on Sundays. This is the time I get to see everyone face-to-face. We get to say our hellos; we get to do a quick check of how everyone is doing; we get donuts or bagels; we give hugs; we go over a few announcements and we pray together. Although this may be quick, we make everyone feel like they're part of a team and there is a connection point for each person each week.

I want to make sure that each person on my team understands that they're valuable to me as a fellow member of God's family first, not only because they're much needed in children's ministry! Their value is in who they are first, and not just in being a volunteer. I make it a priority to spend time with them as we grab coffee, lunch, dinner or do an activity together. Yes, this is a big time commitment. But this time allows me to get to know them on a personal basis. I get to know about their family life, work life, hobbies and even their struggles. As I spend time getting to know them, they also get to know me! And oftentimes, this leads to sharing of my passion and vision for children's ministry. This time has been most meaningful and valuable in connecting with my volunteers. Because I do have a lot of volunteers (and yet never enough), realistically I get to do this 2–4 times a year for every volunteer. I may meet with them individually or in small groups, but I have experienced that the more I get to know them on a personal level, the more likely that they're committed to children's ministry because they start to understand and believe in the vision that I share with them. They also understand that I genuinely love and care for them. They also know that despite their commitment, if they need to take some time off for personal reasons, they can always talk to me, and there won't be any guilt trip for taking time off because I care for them as a person first, and I want them to be healthy!

Everyone on my team receives a birthday greeting from me whether it's via text, postcard, Facebook post, email or phone call (iCal reminder has been integral in helping me with this). When they're absent due to illness or any other events in their lives, I let them know that they're missed and connect with them on whatever is going on in their lives. I do this because I want to lead by example. I tell the volunteers that I want them to be the ones to remember their kids' special events as well as struggles in their lives. How can I expect them to do that for the kids under their care if their leader doesn't do it for them?

We have annual in-house training events where we continually share the vision and values of our ministry, lay out expectations and provide resources that deal with weekly challenges such as discipline or group management. We provide opportunities to attend local or national ministry training events. In fact, we encourage everyone to attend at least one ministry training event per year. This is of value because we often get stuck in what we do in our own church year after year. This provides the opportunity for my volunteers to see how ministry can be done differently and to network with other churches. I email them a serving tip each week—something simple and practical. This serves as a great reminder, and they don't feel like they've been left to sink or swim on their own.

I never expect the volunteers to do anything I wouldn't do myself. I am not above them. I get down and dirty together with them. If we have a VBS decoration preparation day, I don't leave them a list of to-dos. But I roll up my sleeves and join in the fun and work!

I allow volunteers to take initiative and implement their ideas even if it leads to mistakes. I have had some outrageous suggestions come my way, and inside, I cringe. But I use these as teachable opportunities. If their ideas go against our vision or philosophy, I will discuss with them why we wouldn't do as they suggest. Otherwise, I allow them to execute their ideas, and I fully support them (even if I'm cringing on the inside). I do this for a couple reasons. I don't want to discourage them by shooting down their ideas and I don't always know best. Although I don't necessarily think it's the best idea, I want volunteers to initiate and step up. I also believe in allowing people to make mistakes because sometimes, best lessons are learned through mistakes. I journey with them and process with them so we can learn and grow together.

I provide feedback to the volunteers—both positive and negative! Whenever I catch volunteers rising to the occasion (going the extra mile, being patient with challenging kids, etc.), I make it to a point to acknowledge them during the week—once again, a simple email, text, e-card, etc. Words of affirmation go a long way in feeding their souls! Although not as fun, I also have conversations with volunteers regarding what they need to change in their interaction with children—such as their tones, words they use, attitude, etc. I will also redirect volunteers to a different role if we see that he/she isn't a good fit for the current role.

We appreciate and celebrate volunteers! "Thank you" is probably the most uttered phrase on Sundays! "Thank you for serving!" "Thank you for taking the time to talk to Jacob's parents!" "Thank you for being patient with high-energy kids today!" "Thank you for being here early!" "Thank you for all your prep work!" It goes on and on and on. We have appreciation BBQ/pool party in the summer for all children, youth and family ministries volunteers. We have a Christmas party with white elephant gift exchange. We create opportunities to laugh together and say, "We appreciate you and love you!" When you have fun together, people will rearrange their schedules to be there!

This obviously isn't an exhaustive list. Nor is this the only way to lead volunteers. The above ideas are what have worked for me, and also happen to be in line with my style of leading. They also have worked well in our context and size. If we were to grow, I would need another staff member to care for the volunteers with me (I currently have about 25 volunteers). Leading volunteers is no simple job, but it can also be a rewarding one because volunteers directly affect the children we're ministering to! As my passion for children's ministry grows, my passion for leading volunteers well grows. Children's pastors need to invest in their relationship with the volunteers! If church is about bringing people to a growing relationship with Christ and one another, shouldn't that also go for volunteers who serve in our ministries?

Gloria Lee is pastor of children and families at the Jefferson campus of Young Nak Celebration Church in Los Angeles. Connect with her at gloriaslee.wordpress.com.

CHAPTER 32

5 STEPS AND I BIG IDEA TO HELP PARENTS BECOME ALLIES

BY **NAOMI CRAMER OVERTON**

W e sat across the white restaurant table, Jacob and I, guzzling Thai coffee on the first day of the conference. "So you mentioned you lead an organization for families," I started. I'd met Jacob briefly in the midnight hours before when he, seven other ministry leaders, and I smushed into a shuttle from the Bangkok airport to the hotel. Now, alerted by sunlight and caffeine, I wanted to learn more.

Jacob nodded, "My wife and I just started this nonprofit to help families reimagine lives centered around God, each other, and God's world." Jacob's focus sounded like my cup of tea. (Today, however, with a 13-hour-jet-lag, make that strong Thai coffee.)

After serving 100,000 moms a year when I led MOPS (Mothers of Preschoolers) International, and now 1.4 million children annually through Compassion International, I believe in families serving God together. I've marveled at how God has multiplied even our own family's, er, *creative* efforts to show and speak the good news.

Jacob continued with the backstory: "You see, I spent 20 years as a pastor, and week after week parents dropped off their kids, expecting me to give them a dose of God. There were these two kids whose mom I'd almost try to avoid," he laughed apologetically. "If they'd had a spiritual question, she'd come find me saying 'Ask Pastor Jacob. He knows.' I tried helping her answer her own kids' questions, but that didn't work. Eventually, I figured I'd stop playing Answer Man and focus on helping parents live out the pattern of Deuteronomy 6."

As the conference started that evening, the talk of families ceased. For the next four days, 1,000 global church leaders spoke, workshopped, and small-grouped about how to build up children in Christ. Of the presentations, just one—*one of probably 30 talks*—considered the family's role.

During breaks, I'd ask people if they noticed that the topic of families had gone missing. One answered, "Oh, of course parents are the primary spiritual teachers of their children. It's just that they don't respond." Another added. "A lot of parents I've met just lack confidence to guide their kids spiritually." A third offered: "With two-career couples and single moms in the majority, parents just don't have time."

If it's any consolation, these issues go beyond the U-S-of-A. In Compassion's work in Africa, Asia and Latin America, I've visited homes where parents are bussed away to work for days, picking produce. I've been hosted by a lovely teenager, older than her years, whose parents died from HIV-AIDS. And, though many of the 146,000 children a year who accept Christ through a Compassion child development center lead their parents to faith, this kids influencing upwards exists more as a subtext than as the primary biblical imperative.

Parents teaching their kids "on the way" is God's Plan A. But how can parents pass along a faith they lack? A 2008 Barna Research report shows just 3% of Millennials (those born between 1980 and 1993) have a biblical worldview and only about half who left the church after high school will return once they have children.

This article introduces five research-based steps to engaging parents in growing in, and helping their children grow in, the Gospel. It points to others' research plus a 2013 study Barna Research completed for Compassion. This study's six focus groups and nearly 500 surveys showed a pattern of five early steps and one big idea that God works in lives to move parents beyond "Ask Pastor Jacob" mode and into "becoming allies."

STEP #I: TEACH FAMILIES GOD'S PURPOSES.

This includes the kind of teaching popularized by *The Purpose-Driven Life*, teaching that reveals God's broad-brush purpose for humanity as well as fine-tipped calling on our individual lives. As students decide how to maximize school and extracurriculars, parents want to help their kids find their best path. Why not help families discern *God's* path?

STEP #2: TEACH FAMILIES THEY CAN MAKE A DIFFERENCE.

Enabling kids to shape, rather than follow, in serving others affirms they can make a difference and can inspire their parents to join in, too. It may be as simple as what my friend Jonathan recently did with his church: He announced he was going to step back and listen with his student for God to show them ways to serve. His job, rather than defining the service, was to support kids in hearing, and responding, to God's call. Critical to empowering parents to make a difference is coaching them with talking points to discuss with their kids about the meaning behind an upcoming service endeavor.

STEP #3: PERSONALLY INVITE FAMILIES TO DO ONE ACT OF SERVICE.

Willow Creek Association's MOVE study of 1,000 churches and 250,000 individuals found that the "most catalytic action a church can take" to disciple people is to engage them in serving. Similarly, our study showed that mobilized parents had a common experience—some flesh-and-blood individual took them by the arm and said "Hey Scott (or Sally). Let's go serve." Key to this invitation is that it's personal and that it provides one concrete experience children and adults can do together.

STEP #4: SERVE IN FAMILY CLUSTERS.

Consider revamping one kids-or-youth-only missions trip so families gain meaningful roles. If you are not sure this change is worth it, consider this: More people than at any time in history are engaging in short-term missions and yet only two of 13 academically vetted research projects demonstrate quantitative spiritual formation resulting from trips. Conversely, research shows that families who serve together regularly do demonstrate greater discipleship and the longer they serve the more the difference.

STEP #5: SERVE FAMILIES UNLIKE OURS.

While Gannett closed its "MomsLikeMe" bloggers network due to financial priorities in 2011, its rapid growth in 100 markets reminds us how we naturally form tribes with those who mirror us. Author Diana Golding found that serving those unlike our own families stretches, and disciples, us most. As she experienced with her own family, seeing our cultural expectations crash into another family's cultural realities invites us to rely on God, rather than on our own sense of satisfaction.

ONE BIG IDEA: WE SET THE TONE.

So, what one approach underlies this path to helping parents champion kids? It is the leader's (that's your) expectations. Willow Creek's MOVE study found that a leader who regularly sets expectation that everyone (all ages, generations, spiritual maturity levels) has a gift to give, and everyone will be asked to use it, is a leader who's most likely to lead others in spiritual growth. Expect growth, expect service, Willow Creek's study showed, and people will engage.

CONCLUSION: LIVING AS THE HOUSEHOLD OF GOD

We, in this New Testament era, belong to one household (Greek: *oikos*) headed by Jesus: "His purpose was to create in himself one new humanity out of the two ... Consequently you are no longer foreigners and strangers, but fellow citizens with God's people and also members of his household ... with Christ Jesus himself as the chief cornerstone" (Ephesians 2:15–20 NIV).

Oikos in ancient times meant extended families living together, full-time, in buildings we'd describe today as a compound. In our culture, *oikos* has evolved to mean not just a brand of Greek yogurt but *social groups where several hundred people may be known* (think Facebook "friends"), *but the quality time spent with others is extremely limited: only those to whom quality (face-to-face) time is devoted can be said to be a part of an* oikos ... *people who share some sort of social interaction ... for at least a total of one hour per week."*

Similarly, Search Institute's 40 Developmental Assets research shows that children spending one hour a week in a religious gathering are more likely to thrive. A lot of us reading this are face-to-face with kids for one hour a week, as are Compassion's child development center staff who kids see four to eight hours weekly or more.

So that's good news: By modern terms, most of us are already part of kids' households, their *oikos*. Though we may be the equivalent of Uncle Bob or Aunt Betty who arrive once a week for an awkward dinner, we have a foothold to influence the regulars toward togetherness under household head, Jesus. By taking steps, such as the five listed here, and embracing the big idea of *expecting generations to serve together*, let's invite parents to become allies and whole families to thrive in Jesus' *oikos*, his Plan A: God's new humanity.

Naomi Cramer Overton is Compassion International's USA Advocacy Director. Prior to joining Compassion, she served as President and CEO of MOPS International. Naomi is married to her college sweetheart, Frank. They have three children and a dog named Coco Loco.

CHAPTER 33

WHY KIDS WORSHIP IS WORTH IT

BY BOB SINGLETON

We were in the studio, working on our new Christmas album when we started rehearsing my kids chorus. It's my favorite time in the studio, working with a group of terrific 8 to 12-year-old studio singers. We were looking through lyrics for the first time while we listened to the music tracks. I watched as they concentrated, their lips moving, their brows furrowed and their toes and fingers dancing to "Deck the Hall," a song they'd be recording later that day.

Suddenly, Erin, one of my 11-year-old girl singers, straightened up and pointed at her lyrics. "Wait!" she exclaimed, her face filled with surprise and confusion.

"'See the blazing YULE before us?'" she demanded. "I always thought the words were, 'See the blazing MULE before us!'"

That stopped everything. We laughed until we wept; our noses ran, and our sides hurt. What a mental image! We made jokes about fire-roasting mules through the rest of production, adding precious minutes of recording studio time to the budget, but making memories for a lifetime.

WORTH IT TO BUILD LIFE FOUNDATIONS

I can still feel and remember the laughter, snickering conversations, joy and friendship and the physical sensations of that day attached to eight simple notes from the first line of that song.

I think that is why God exhorts us in Psalm 47:6–7 (NET Bible):

Sing to God! Sing!

Sing to our king! Sing!

For God is king of the whole earth!

Sing a well-written song!

Isn't it amazing how God has created us to recall more than just the words that are attached to songs? God has uniquely wired people, and especially kids, to be touched mind, soul and body by songs. Children tuck away the concepts, feelings and words of songs in their hearts and minds for a lifetime. God wants your kids to sing to Him in worship! Kids are wired and ready to sing. We should sing "well-written songs," but we don't have to sing well! We just need to make our "joyful noise" to the Lord, no matter what age we are. God never expresses age or talent limits for worshiping Him; He just wants us to be enthusiastic, as written later in the Psalms:

Let everything that has breath praise the Lord! (Psalms 150:6 NET Bible)

Every kid in children's ministry today has breath. Start kids praising and worshiping when they are young, and keep it growing as they grow. It lays a foundation for a lifetime of communing with God.

In kids worship, the first priority is to connect kids to God. If your kids are connected to God, you have the ability to teach and disciple them deeply in ways you've never imagined. Worship is rarely the act of singing songs that are designed simply to teach. Teaching is the act of pouring information into kids' minds. Worship is the act of pouring love and adoration into the arms of our loving, listening God.

As children's ministry workers, we lead kids to Christ, and fill them with information about God. But do we help them to encounter God? Do we put that off until they get into youth programs, or "grown-up" church? More people become Christians as children than any other age group, but experience leads me to think that a smaller percentage of children worship than any other age group.

What are those non-worshiping kids missing? They could be missing the planting of foundational concepts that will enrich their lives into eternity. Jan Bedell, a neat Christian mom and overachiever whose credentials include B.S, M.ND, M.Ed, Certified Teacher, Certified Master Neurodevelopmentalist, plus founder and President of Little Giant Steps says,

When a person memorizes something that is put to music, it is stored in the subdominant hemisphere of the brain, where emotions and creativity take place. This information is permanently stored and easy to retrieve when sung. It's been observed that information that is memorized to music lasts the longest, and is the last to be forgotten. Even Alzheimer's patients can often retrieve songs from their childhood when other information has been lost.

WORTH IT AS MULTI-SENSE EXPERIENCE

Kids are more wired for music than grown-ups. They respond faster, memorize it faster, and sense the emotion and energy more deeply than adults. We hear that kids are "multi-sensory" learners. Singing is one of the most multi-sensory activities that we can undertake, and it can be done anywhere. As children grow and become more dominant in their learning styles, some aspect of singing will always reach them, whether it's thinking about the words, enjoying the physical movement, or thriving on the creative aspects of music.

Jody Capehart, experienced children's pastor and school administrator, and author of the gold medallion-nominated book *Teaching with Heart* says,

Brain research supports that children are multi-sensory learners. They learn best and retain more when information is presented through multi-modalities. Motor stimulation, which can include activities required for singing, activates the neural connections in the brain to facilitate learning and long-term memory. Many children learn best when they are moving because they build in muscle memory. Music and movement provide an excellent combination for worship and scripture memory.

Worship singing is a multi-sensory experience that affects our body, soul and mind:

- Bodies: We tap our feet, clap our hands and change our heartbeat and breathing when we sing. We see others singing, we hear the sounds, we feel the vibrations of our voice, the touch of the floor and the impact of our hands clapping.

- Souls: Our souls and emotions are touched as we are reminded of all that God has done for us, and all His amazing promises.

- Minds: Our mind is fed with eternal truth about God that continues to feed us for life. The truths we learn in song return to our conscious minds when we need them most for the rest of our life.

God wants our expressions of love for Him to involve our whole being. In Mark 12:30, Jesus reminds us how we are to express our love for God:

> Love the Lord your God with all your heart, with all your soul, with all your mind, and with all your strength. (NET Bible)

Singing praise to our God encompasses all of those actions. How much of the time with your kids is devoted to connecting them with God through worship? It doesn't take much; just 5 to 15 minutes is all that's needed. How much richer will their spiritual walk be, if they can connect with God in singing praise? Try it and see!

WORTH IT WORSHIP LOOKS LIKE

We often try to make worship more difficult than it's meant to be. It doesn't require a certain setting or special training. Worship is simply telling back to God his "worth-ship," or worthiness, that He is worth anything and everything. Contemporary worship leader and songwriter Matt Redman says, "To worship God is to tell Him that we believe Him for who He says He is." (Matt and Beth Redman, *Blessed Be Your Name* pub. Regal Books.)

Developmentally, kids connect with God as He is revealed in their world. Their ability to grasp God grows as their perception of the world around them grows. Smaller kids, whose world is the size of their family and the current room they are in, will be able to worship God for His actions and presence in those things. As kids develop and their world expands, they are able to worship God for His actions in the world that fits their developmental awareness. Go for content that fits the size of their world, but don't be afraid to introduce "bigger picture" concepts that the Spirit will use to help them grow later. "Yes, Jesus Loves Me" contains huge theological implications, but God is able to fit that concept, which is as big as the universe and all time, into the heart of a child.

Your choice of music should fit the worship style and theology of your church. Look for music with enough energy to match the energy level of your kids. Whatever your church's worship style, expect kids to be kids, and use kid-appropriate worship songs. The Bible doesn't describe any particular musical style for worship, but looking at Psalm 150, it seems OK to be noisy!

Select proven worship songs and energized hymns that fit the voices and developmental stage for kids in the room. Don't be afraid to use many of the same songs you sing in "big church" that fit their vocal ranges and temperament. Kids shouldn't go into culture shock when they attend the adult service.

Our studies of collected research indicate that kids up through around 6th grade prefer to sing along with kids voices over adults; it's easy to "fit in" when they sing, and these are more likely to be in their vocal range. Songs that work best are not too long, usually two to four minutes. Find and use energetic arrangements, but don't be afraid to let kids dig in to worship with range-and-content-appropriate slow songs. Sing slower songs after two or three energized ones, and fit their attention span. Present teaching or prayer time after a slower song, when you've got your kids in a quieter, focused place.

WORSHIP—BLESSINGS IN RETURN

When kids worship God, He is pleased by their worship. Colossians 33:16 says, "With thankful hearts we sing psalms, hymns, and spiritual songs to God." As our kids give their worship to God, He gives back to them blessings that fill them with thankfulness.

Matt Redman in the foreword to *I Could Sing of Your Love Forever* published by Regal Books says, "Our worship songs are for Jesus—yet as they work their way out of our hearts and toward heaven, they so often work wonders in us."

Lead your kids into worship. It's not hard, and it starts with singing. And, great news! God doesn't require good voices, just enthusiastic hearts:

Praise him with the blast of the horn!

Praise him with the lyre and the harp!

Praise him with the tambourine and with dancing!

Praise him with stringed instruments and the flute!

Praise him with loud cymbals!

Praise him with clanging cymbals!

Let everything that has breath praise the Lord!

Psalms 150: 3-6 (NET Bible)

Bob Singleton is President of God's Kids Worship™ (godskidsworship.com), making kids worship DVDs and downloadable files for churches of all sizes. He's also a kids worship ministry consultant, and platinum album award-winning, Grammy and Dove-nominated producer of music for kids.

CHAPTER 34

JANE AUSTEN'S TAKE ON CURRICULUM

BY LINDA WEDDLE

Hmm ... what? Well, the famous 19th century English novelist was a rector's daughter. Her dad supplemented his income by tutoring young boys, so she probably knew a thing or two about curriculum.

But even if Jane didn't understand scope and sequence, we do know she was familiar with the curricle. The two-wheeled chariot was big enough for a couple and drawn by a pair of horses. The curricle was most popular during the early 19th century. Many of Jane's dashing male characters drove such a cart, considered the sports car of its day.

So what's a curricle have to do with curriculum? The word *curricle* actually comes from the Latin word *curriculum. Curriculum* literally means running or racecourse. That makes sense when applied to Jane's chariot but takes a little more thought when applied to a pattern of study.

Curriculum originally referred to the events and experiences that made up a child's life both within a structured learning environment and outside of that environment. John Franklin Bobbitt (1918) was one of the first authors to write a book about curriculum, creatively called *The Curriculum.* In the book, he expounds on the idea that curriculum is a racecourse comprised of all facets of a child's life as he matures into an adult.

We now think of curriculum as an isolated course of study rather than everything a child experiences. To many in ministry, curriculum is simply that packet of info—the teacher's book, the handouts and the craft supplies—distributed at the beginning of each year of service. The teacher is concerned that all the parts are there (and whether he'll have time to prepare between soccer coaching, work and getting the garage painted). He's not considering how the material fits into the curriculum of a child's life.

Are we on a life course with our curriculum? I think of the children's education meeting I recently attended. I listened to several staff members discuss a change in curriculum. The conversation went something like this:

- Teacher 1—We used Publisher A's curriculum for our summer program last year and had a lot of success, but I think it takes too much preparation.

- Teacher 2—We could use Publisher B. They have a space theme this year. Kids like planets, rockets and astronauts.

- Teacher 3—We used space for our Sunday morning program just two years ago.

- Teacher 2—Publisher C has great activities and fantastic graphics on take-home papers, but they're shallow and even infer that the Bible is not the inspired Word of God.

- Teacher 3 (skimming through a book)—Look at these cute, edible arks.

The conversation continued for another hour or so, but I don't have to repeat it. You've probably been there and done that. In other words, curriculum choice was based on a plan that didn't take much effort, had a never-been-done-before theme and lots of recipes for cute snacks.

When planning our next year (or the next 5–10 years) in our children's ministries, we need to move beyond themes, colors and marshmallow arks. We need to get back to the basics. We must prayerfully choose curriculum that stays on course and involves all areas of a child's life.

We need to look at curriculum in terms of life context.

CURRICULUM—A COURSE FOR A CHILD'S LIFE

Next June, when your class of 6-year-olds takes a break for the summer, what biblically-centered life knowledge do you want them to have? Is your goal that they'll be able to make toothpick mangers? Or that they'll know the nine segments of the fruit of the Spirit backwards and forwards (and, in the case of gymnastics-loving Kaylee, standing on her head)?

But let's go further. Do you want them to know how those nine qualities apply to their lives and to their parents' lives and to everything they do? Do you want to draw in the parents and have love, joy and peace also practiced in their home?

You might have this plan in place. More and more churches are developing not only year-long plans, but 5- or 10-year plans. The curriculum is solid. Scope and sequences have been written. Scope is your direction and the goals you have in place to get there. Sequence is the way you want your lessons to fit together to meet those goals.

Yet many churches do not have such plans. They stumble along year by year, choosing the easiest-to-teach curriculum with an overabundance of fun, non-essential activities. Even state-of-the-art educational tools are worthless if they teach nothing.

Does your church have a life-course outline for the children in your ministry? If not, suggest that your children's ministry leadership put such a plan in place. If you cannot convince your children's pastor that such a plan is important, then start one yourself. Yes, the plan would be more valuable if all teachers and departments worked together. But that doesn't mean you can't work on one for the year (or for the two or three years) you plan the lessons for your department. Make sure you have clear goals for the lessons you teach.

Write down what you want to accomplish. Put down five (or 10) central truths that you want your students to know by next summer. Teach those truths. Review those truths. Live those truths.

Prayerfully ask for wisdom in carrying out your church's children's ministry goals or in establishing your own goals for your class.

CURRICULUM—A COURSE FOR RIGHT NOW, THIS MINUTE

We need to get serious. Children spend approximately 1,146 hours in school each year and another 2,190 hours in screen time. How much time do we have? If our program is an hour a week, that's 52 hours, minus the seven hours they miss for sickness or because their family is out of town. If we work in a program that coincides with the school year, those hours are cut down to 30. Thirty hours is not a lot of time to accomplish our life-course curriculum goals. Paul wrote in Ephesians 5:16, "Redeeming the time, because the days are evil." The English Standard Version translates "redeeming" as "making the best use of."

We need to be aware of our long-term plan. But we also need to be intentionally focused during each lesson. Is the opening activity a time when children play with blocks also an opportunity for teachers to chat with the children, letting them know that they're interested in their lives? Or is the opening free time for the teachers to stand in the back of the room and discuss last night's game or a new cupcake recipe?

Is the craft activity a random shape covered with glitter? Or a paper scroll to show what "books" looked like or another piece of furniture for the model tabernacle the class is making?

During the large group lesson, are teachers sitting with their children? Or is this an opportunity for all but the teacher giving the lesson to escape to the church kitchen for some coffee?

The finished lesson is the ultimate goal, but we get there step by step, redeeming the time.

CURRICULUM—A COURSE FOR ALL AREAS OF LIFE

If curriculum is based on a whole-life course, then we want the child's whole life included. Sometimes we can do that. Sometimes we can't. Ideally, children's ministry supports what the child is being taught at home. In another instruction to the Ephesians, Paul writes in Ephesians 6:4 that the father is "to bring them up in the training and admonition of the Lord." Moms also greatly influence children. Look at Timothy and the scripture he learned from his mother and grandmother.

As teachers we need to connect with the parents. That could be by inviting them to observe the class, sending home family study guides or communicating through blogs, Twitter or Facebook. But let's be realistic. Yes, a lot of parents are connecting with what we're teaching. But many have no idea about our curriculum goals even though we've emailed, sent home information with their children and invited them to parents' meetings. Nothing seems to make a difference.

This is all the more reason we need to focus on curriculum for life. We need to role-play how children should act in different situations, do object lessons or tell stories to teach kids life application. In addition, we need to teach by the way we live our everyday lives. Draw the parents in to what you're teaching so their children truly are taught an everyday-life curriculum.

As Catherine (Jane Austen's heroine of *Northanger Abbey*) was riding along in dashing Henry Tilney's curricle, she said it made her "as happy a being as ever existed." The goal of curriculum goes further than that. We desire to biblically direct our children in a Christ-centered life course.

 Linda Massey Weddle is the senior program specialist at Awana. She has been active in children's ministry for more than 30 years and is the author of 13 books, the most recent *How to Raise a Modern-Day Joseph.*

CHAPTER 35

HONEY I SHRUNK THE GOSPEL

BY **SAM LUCE**

I n 1989, Rick Moranis entered into the vernacular of our culture with the words, "Honey, I shrunk the kids." Moranis portrays a wacky inventor who accidentally shrinks his kids and the neighbor kids with the shrink ray he invented. Moranis' character is unaware that his kids were shrunk by the very invention he destroys, because he thinks it doesn't work. There were multiple spin-offs of the movie and "Honey, I shrunk the (fill in the blank with something witty)" became a staple of sitcoms for most of the 90s.

A very real and dangerous problem in the church today is the fact that we have simplified, truncated and made the Gospel powerless in our churches and in our homes. Honey, we have shrunk the Gospel!

What is the Gospel? Terms matter and many people refer to the Gospel, but I'm not sure that we're always talking about the same thing. The Gospel is the good news. It's the good news that we have been longing to hear since God created a perfect world that we messed up when we introduced sin into it. Because we have sinned and have broken God's perfect world, He had to send His sinless Son to live the life we could not live, to die a death we should have died. Jesus came back to life, ascended into heaven and will come back to make right all the things that are wrong about our world. That is the good news in a nutshell. We don't have to be good enough, because Jesus is, was and continues to be our spotless sacrifice.

SO HOW HAVE WE SHRUNK THE GOSPEL?

We have oversimplified the Gospel.

We make the Gospel small when we oversimplify it to our kids. In our desire to make the Gospel simple, we inadvertently rob the Gospel of its power. We tell our kids what Christians do, rather than who Christ is. We talk about how God loves us, but fail to tell them how He demonstrated that to us in Christ.

It's very easy to simplify the Gospel through pat answers. When our kids ask meaningful questions, we must wade into the complex. If we simplify truth to our kids, the danger is that we can satisfy God-given wonder with a simple, practical truth. We give our kids enough of Jesus that we inoculate them from the whole of the Gospel. They come to believe that this watered-down version of the Gospel is all there is, and because it has been simplified and watered down, it has no application in our daily lives.

It's equally easy to teach our kids moral truth, because the lines are clear and the outcome is desirable. We want them to demonstrate the moral attributes of God. But if we oversimplify the Gospel into a simple moral truth, we fail to accomplish what God desires from us. He doesn't want good citizens who do good things. God wants us to be joyful. He wants us to get the joy so He can get the glory.

When we oversimplify the Gospel, we shrink its influence on every aspect of our lives.

We have made the Gospel about salvation alone.

We have so condensed the Gospel that we've made it about what Jesus did on Easter. What Jesus did in dying for us is essential, and kids need to hear that part of the message loud and clear. But what gives that message so much power is understanding the context of the broader story of the creation, fall, redemption and restoration. We teach our kids believing the Gospel is the moment they raise their hands at VBS. They check the salvation box and then move on from the Gospel to the "more important truths." We must teach our kids that they are part of a story that God has been writing since the beginning. They have a part and must engage the story God is writing in and through them with the broader story of the salvation and redemption of mankind.

We shrink the Gospel when we focus on a part and fail to tell the whole beautiful story of it.

We buy into Gospel = Lemonade.

In kids' ministry, we easily fall victim to a Gospel that is socially active. We encourage kids to sell lemonade and give the money to the poor. Again, this is something that's important for our kids to learn but deadly for them to trust in for ultimate joy and hope. *You must make sure that our social action is coming from a deep conviction and personal gratitude for what Jesus did for you, not as a way to score brownie points with the Trinity.* I do good things for Him; therefore, I expect good things from Him.

"Let your light shine before men in such a way that they may see your good works, and glorify your Father who is in heaven" (Matthew 5:16). Love this verse. The purpose of our service is His glory. Jesus continues on in the next couple of chapters explaining how we are powerless to fulfill the Law, but how the Law is to humble us, to help us see the need to be rescued.

When so great a Savior has rescued us, the natural response of our hearts is gratitude. We can love Him and love others, because He first loved us.

We shrink the Gospel when we believe social justice is the goal of the Christian life, rather than a by-product of a Gospel-centered Christian life.

Jesus and Me.

I'm not sure I've ever met anyone who grew up in church who didn't learn the simple song "Jesus Loves Me This I Know." Understanding that Jesus loves you is massively important and foundational to your faith. Where this powerful truth can shrink our faith is at the moment we over-personalize our faith.

In the United States, we tend to highly value rugged individualism. We have personal entertainment devices and all the modern trappings that allow us to have everything that make life more comfortable. For this comfort, we pay a high price. We lose the relationships that God has placed in our lives to help mold us into the image of His Son.

The individualism in the Western church has done much damage. We have a personal Savior, personal prayer time, personal devotions, personal, personal, personal. The problem with Jesus being our personal Savior and Lord is we tend to isolate ourselves from the community aspect where our faith was meant to thrive. I don't believe that you can fully understand forgiveness, repentance and redemption outside of the context of community. If you want to grow in your faith, you have to do that in community.

C.S. Lewis describes the value of knowing others and being known by others in his book *The Four Loves*. Lewis was part of a group of three men who had a very strong friendship. One of the members of the group, Charles, suddenly died and Lewis found himself sad, yet somewhat happy, because he would have more of the time and attention of his other friend, Ronald Tolkien. Lewis tells us of how misguided his thoughts were:

> *In each of my friends there is something that only some other friend can fully bring out. By myself I am not large enough to call the whole man into activity; I want other lights than my own to show all his facets. Now that Charles is dead, I shall never again see Ronald's [Tolkien's] reaction to a specifically Charles joke. Far from having more of Ronald, having him 'to myself' now that Charles is away, I have less of Ronald ... In this, Friendship exhibits a glorious 'nearness by resemblance' to heaven itself where the very multitude of the blessed (which no man can number) increases the fruition which each of us has of God. For every soul, seeing Him in her own way, doubtless communicates that unique vision to all the rest. That, says an old author, is why the Seraphim in Isaiah's vision are crying 'Holy, Holy, Holy' to one another (Isaiah 6:3). The more we thus share the Heavenly Bread between us, the more we shall have.*

It takes a whole community to fully know an individual. If this is true of us, how much more true is it of Christ? There are many aspects of the reality of Christ and the depths of the Gospel that will never be fully realized alone. We must be in a community of faith to walk out the Gospel together.

When we shrink the Gospel down to "me and Jesus," we minimize the impact of the Gospel on our lives and the lives of countless others who need to hear the Gospel preached and see the Gospel lived.

> *All we can say, therefore, is: the community of Christians spring solely from the biblical and reformation message of the justification of man through grace alone; this alone is the basis for the longing of Christians for one another. (Dietrich Bonhoeffer)*

We must act, we must love, we must do all that we can for Jesus, but all of that must come from an understanding of what

God has done for us in Christ and in a community of believers or it will simply be our goodness minus the Gospel. The good news for us is found in 1 Timothy 1:15–17:

> *It is a trustworthy statement, deserving full acceptance, that Christ Jesus came into the world to save sinners, among whom I am foremost of all. Yet for this reason I found mercy, so that in me as the foremost, Jesus Christ might demonstrate His perfect patience as an example for those who would believe in Him for eternal life. Now to the King eternal, immortal, invisible, the only God, be honor and glory forever and ever. Amen.*

If we view our lives in light of our accomplishments, rather than what Jesus has done for us, we shrink the Gospel and its power in our lives.

Sam Luce is the Campus Pastor at Redeemer Church in Utica, NY. He's most passionate about glorifying God in every area of his life. Married to his lovely wife for 15 years, together their family is far from shrinking as they welcome a fourth child. He blogs at samluce.com.

CHAPTER 36

THE SQUIRREL SYNDROME
BY **RON BROOKS**

We are big Disney movie fans at our house. One very fun movie that we may not watch often but we reference all the time is the movie *UP*. We loved the movie, and all the time we find ourselves yelling "SQUIRREL!" If you have not seen the movie, there is a talking dog named Dug who becomes easily distracted. In mid-conversation he will stop and point, in the way only a dog could do, and he yells "squirrel" as if he is ready to take off in pursuit of a squirrel. "Squirrel" has become synonymous with becoming distracted or losing focus. I don't know about you, but I encounter quite a few squirrel moments when teaching kids.

Speaking to kids is much different than teaching and speaking to adults. An adult usually has the self-control to sit and listen, even when not interested. A child, no matter the age, does not possess that same skill. They may be able to sit for a few minutes, but if they aren't interested, you will soon know it. If you find yourself presented with the opportunity to teach children, whether in a classroom, a library, a small group, a ministry, a Sunday School or you name the setting, there are a few things I have learned over the years that could be beneficial.

It is important to remember that everyone learns differently. The fact is most of us will teach the way that we learn best. The problem with that is there will always be kids you are dealing with who learn differently. If you are not prepared to vary your methods, you can be sure you will lose many of them. And we all know what happens once a child is no longer interested. Let the discipline issues begin!

There are many tips and tricks you could employ, but here a few examples of what has worked for me.

I. ENGAGE THE EYES

There are kids who are visual learners. They learn by what they see. Use props when you teach or speak. Give the kids something to look at other than you. I am sure you think you can be interesting enough, but they see you all the time. Do an object lesson or an experiment to help make your point. Use a costume. Show a photo. Give them something else to look at. Even kids who are not visual learners will pay better attention when there are cool things to look at.

One of my favorite ways to engage visual learners is with a costume. Sometimes that means I use a hat or a shirt to help make a point. Other times I use a full costume in an attempt to become a character. Teddy, an obnoxious five-year-old is one of my favorite characters.

Teddy's costume is brightly colored, and he moves a lot. Sometimes he even sits with the kids. The fun thing about Teddy (or any other character) is that the kids are so engaged with the action and conversation that they are hanging on every word that is spoken, and they can't wait to see what happens next. Because Teddy is able to engage their eyes, it is very easy for them to focus and pay attention, but better yet, they learn the lesson of the morning right along with Teddy.

Costumed characters are just one tool for you to use. Whether a costume or something else, do your best to engage the eyes.

2. ENGAGE THE EARS

One trick I am sure most of you know is to vary the volume of your voice. I have found that when kids start to check out and talk among themselves and not pay attention, that is a good time to lower your voice and make it harder to hear you. Often those kids listening will tell the loud kids to be quiet so everyone can hear. Or the kids who are not paying attention will stop and try to listen, because it gets their attention because you are quieter. It works the other way as well.

While he is funny, and dressed brightly, Teddy is also loud. It is actually hard to not pay attention to him when he is around. Maybe you choose a character who is very quiet, like a librarian. When kids (or adults for that matter) are trying to listen, they are very focused on listening and understanding what is being spoken. You can take advantage of this by varying your volume.

You don't have to have a character though to make use of volume. Don't be afraid to get loud, or even yell. Especially when there is an exciting part in your story. Be excited! I have startled many kids with a well-timed yell during teaching time. It definitely works to get everyone's attention.

Whether you are loud or quiet, be conscious of your volume. Doing so will be sure to engage the ears.

3. ENGAGE THE BODY

There is lots of research that says some kids learn better when they move. I have often used hand motions when teaching new vocabulary words. If you don't believe me, what do you do with your hands when I say "the itsy bitsy spider" or "patty cake patty cake"? Movement helps us remember. It is easy to find ways to allow the kids to move during a lesson or a story. Have them raise their hand or stand up when they hear you say a key word. One of my favorite types of movement is to have kids act out part of your story as you tell it. Ask questions and have them move to different parts of the room based on what they think the answer is. Find a way to add some movement into your lesson or story.

Each week we have a video-based peanut butter and jelly race, in which peanut butter, bread and jelly race on the screen. I am able to control the winner, so the kids never know which racer will win. Before the race begins, I have the kids move to a certain part of the room based on who they think will win.

Some high energy praise and worship time also serves a dual purpose: allowing a time to dance and praise, while at the same time giving kids a chance to move around and get wiggles out, which will help them focus better when it is time to sit and listen.

Remember movement often assists learning, so engage the body.

4. ENGAGE THE MIND

You are teaching or telling stories for the sake of having the kids learn. To help solidify the concepts or ideas you are teaching, be sure to ask questions. Have them retell part of the story in their own words. Ask open-ended questions that make them think instead of just recite what they heard. Be sure to engage their mind.

Like I said, there are many other things you can do to become a better teacher or storyteller. This is just a short list of things everyone can do to become better. Our goal is the same—to help kids learn. When we remember that kids learn differently, we can change our teaching strategy to be more effective in reaching those different learning styles.

Not only will this help you become a better teacher, and help kids learn, you will also reduce the behavior issues. When kids are actively listening and learning, they are less likely to act up. Not only are you being a better teacher or telling a better story, you are stopping many behavior issues that result from simple boredom.

 Ron Brooks is children's ministry pastor at New Generations Church in Canton, Michigan. Connect with him at ikidsonline. org or on Twitter at @ronbrooks77.

CHAPTER 37

THE PURITY AND POWER OF WORSHIP

BY YANCY

Have you ever experienced a group of kids worshipping? I mean really worshipping: eyes closed, hands lifted, voices singing loud and strong? I truly believe it is one of the sweetest sounds you could ever hear in this whole world. I know on many occasions I have been moved to tears and taken aback by the purity, sweetness and honor that shines in those precious moments. I might be the one leading a group of kids in worship, but when that special thing happens when creation worships the Creator—I stand there reminded of the greatness of our God.

There are a lot of lessons that we as adults can learn from a group of kids worshipping. An example of childlike faith perfectly demonstrated. God created us to worship Him and from what I've found, it's a pretty natural and easy thing for kids to

261

worship. Kids are by far the easiest age group to lead in worship. They are much easier to lead than any middle-aged man in big church or the hardest of hearts in your congregation. I treasure a picture I have of my one-and-a-half-year-old-son taking part in worship during a summer camp where I was helping lead worship. At that point, he hadn't been taught how to do it. He had not gone to a "baby worship school." It is just naturally in us to worship the One who made us and knows every detail of our lives. I came across a verse that transformed how I look at kids worship. It's not just singing songs; it's filled with power. Take a look at Psalm 8:1–2:

> *God, brilliant Lord, yours is a household name. Nursing infants gurgle choruses about you; toddlers shout the songs that drown out enemy talk, and silence atheist babble.*
> *(MSG)*

From the youngest nursery class to the oldest preteen you minister to, their praises are power-filled and can make someone who doesn't even believe in God change their mind and believe our God is real. Think about that for a minute. That is powerful. Kids worshipping God is a powerful thing. It's time to stop neglecting that kind of power from going forth in our ministry each week.

There are many things that our kids will experience in the various classrooms and programs of your church throughout their childhood. There are many lessons, Bible verses and themes that will be repeated. And yes, it's important kids learn about loving one another, missions, obeying their parents and amazing stories like Noah, David and what Jesus did on the cross for us. Just like those important lessons that no doubt will get taught, if we want to end up with teenagers and adults who know how to worship the Jesus they are living for, then we must give kids an opportunity to worship now. You might say, oh we do that in our classes already. Really? Do you give kids an opportunity to have praise and worship each week in their class? Are you intentional with the time? Do you just sing silly songs that are activity-based? What have you taught them about why you worship, why you sing, clap or even lift your hands? Are they expected to be reverent and behave a certain way during this time? Or is it a free for all, anything goes, 12–15 minute time killer that looks like a tornado touching down?

I'm not trying to be hard or harsh in my questions. I am however passionate about kids learning that they can worship, now! God delights in our praises. Psalm 92:1–2 says:

It is good to praise the Lord and make music to your name, O Most High, proclaiming your love in the morning and your faithfulness at night (NIV).

Worshipping God is a good thing. It's something that will only help the kids you minister to deepen their foundation in Christ. Praising God plants seeds of faith in our heart for how great God is. I know my Christian faith has been impacted because of songs that I learned as a kid. Those biblical truths were planted in my spirit. The more I sang them, the more they took root and started to grow. As I live out my life even now, I can't help but be reminded of the impact that those songs made on my view that God does what He says He'll do.

Think through the songs you sing and why you're doing them. They are more than just slots to fill on your planning sheet for the day. Is it more than just a music time or a way to fill up minutes of the time that you have "watching" the kids? In my experiences of travelling and talking to leaders from all over, I realize that we have a lot of work to do in this area. Very few churches I've found are being intentional about giving kids an opportunity to worship and teaching them how to do it. I am burdened to shine a spotlight on this subject and help leaders take some steps to transform from just singing silly songs to having a fun, engaging time that honors and lifts high the name of the Lord. Did you notice I said, "take some steps." I sure hope so, because it's not a one-size-fits-all remedy where you're going to do a couple new things this week and completely change the attitude and landscape of what worship is for your kids. It will take steps, time and diligence. It may be a process (especially the older the child is) but, I can promise you, if you will take those steps, invest some time and be diligent, you will see a transformation. What worship looks like in your KidMin three, six, nine and twelve months from now can be a totally different thing from where you are today.

Questions to ask yourself to evaluate the relevancy of what you're currently doing:

- What does your music sound like?
- Who do you have on stage leading worship?
- Do your leaders look like they like to worship?
- How have you taught kids about worship?
- On a scale of one to ten, how well do the kids participate?

Questions to ask yourself for where you want to go:

- What do you want to see accomplished in the hearts of your kids in regards to worship?
- Define that for each classroom/age group in your ministry.
- How can each class build upon the next?
- What are ways, each week, you can teach why and how we worship?

You need to find a leader(s) who has a passion for this area, who can help lead kids in this area. That person may be you or it may be someone else. But, I know that just pressing play on a DVD and relying on the video is only going to get you so far. We need a person coaching us and encouraging us. Have you ever been on a sports team or worked out with a trainer? That person standing over us encouraging us to do the workout is what keeps us motivated and accountable to do it. We've all been there before where when working out on our own we decide "that's good enough," and take a rain check of what we should have done. That coach saying "You can do it," "Three more times," "C'mon, you got this" is what inspires us to continue when our body wants to give up. When it comes to worship leading, it's the same way. We are encouraging good behavior. The worship leader isn't asking you to do something that's harmful or spiritually bad. No, it's a good thing! (Psalm 92:1 taught us that.) It takes the worship leader saying "C'mon, clap your hands," "Sing it again," "Sing it louder," or "One more time" to encourage the participation for us to do the good thing that is worshipping the Lord. That's why a video is never going to completely do worship leading for you. You need someone who can carry the transitions, gauge how your group is doing and say things to inspire, encourage and teach them.

Here's some practical ways you can teach and lead worship for any age group:

- Share scriptures about praise and the greatness of God and why we should worship. We were made in His image. Just like we enjoy hearing compliments said about us, God is the same way. He loves when we worship Him. Our worship is a way we can compliment God on who He is, what He has done and let Him know what He means to us.

- Teach about biblical examples like David who worshipped the Lord unashamed with boldness!

- Be energetic. It's okay to have fun! God smiles when we praise Him. Celebrate!

- Lead on their level. State the obvious. Kids are used to being told what to do. Plus, we all need reminders from time to time. Tell the kids to sing, clap their hands, lift their hands, put a smile on their faces, sing from their hearts, etc.

- Be consistent; remember you are there to coach them in praising God. If you have different people leading from week to week or you have multiple services, it's important to coach your team to all lead in the same way so you don't have one class really excel in this area and another one not so much. Kids figure out who expects what and then adjust their behavior. Set the bar and keep it there.

- Ask questions that demand a response. This is one of the easiest things you can do to engage your group.

- Be an example of worship yourself. Demonstrate through your actions, words and countenance what it looks like. Also, when you attend a service you need to be a worshiper. Don't just expect others to do it when you're the leader. Worship when others are leading you. (Sowing and reaping!)

Our example matters.

Our time matters.

Our words matter.

Look at these verses in Psalm 145:3–7:

Great is the Lord and most worthy of praise;

his greatness no one can fathom.

One generation commends your works to another;

they tell of your mighty acts.

They speak of the glorious splendor of your majesty—

and I will meditate on your wonderful works.

They tell of the power of your awesome works—

and I will proclaim your great deeds.

They celebrate your abundant goodness

and joyfully sing of your righteousness (NIV).

These verses show us the importance of parents teaching and showing their kids how to worship. If you are a parent, then think about that and start demonstrating this to your own kids at home. But, even in this ministry we are doing to lead kids in worship we are spiritual parents to the kids there. I believe if we take this instruction from Psalm 145 to heart, your kids' ministry worship can go to new places you've never been. Amazing things are ahead in the weeks and months to come. I believe a new generation is rising up to proclaim the majesty, miracles and great things God has done. Music is an amazing tool that we have to connect and communicate with kids. It's also an amazing tool we can give them to connect and communicate with their Heavenly Father. Start investing now in the kids and families you serve. Show and teach others how to worship the living and true God that we serve. All praise, honor and glory are His forevermore!

Yancy is a worship leader and songwriter for kids. She recently released *Roots for the Journey* a scripture-based worship album and family devotional app. Her life is made even more complete with her husband, Cory and son, Sparrow Rocket. Connect with her at YancynotNancy.com.

CHAPTER 38

PRAY ABOUT IT

BY **KEITH FERRIN**[9]

I don't pray for my kids enough. There...I said it. I know I should. I certainly want them to grow up knowing and loving God and His Word. And I know the Word tells me that, through prayer, I have access to the very Throne Room of the Almighty. And yet, I don't pray for my kids nearly enough. How about you?

I am convinced that prayer is essential if the next generation is going to grow in their love and knowledge of the Word. This chapter is not going to explore all the different ways we can pray for our children. There are many tremendous books already written on that subject. I simply want to lay out four areas where prayer is vital when it comes to the next generation falling in love with God's Word.

PRAY FOR GOD TO DRAW THEM.

In John 6, Jesus is talking to a pretty hostile crowd. Understandable, since He's talking to a crowd about being the "bread of life,"

9. "This chapter is one of the nine principles Keith Ferrin explores in his book *Like Ice Cream (The Scoop on Helping the Next Generation Fall in Love with God's Word)*

coming down from the Father, eating His flesh, and drinking His blood! In the middle of this conversation (verse 44) He says, "No one can come to me unless the Father who sent me draws him." Jesus must be pretty serious about this, because 21 verses later – as the crowd is getting increasingly hostile – He says again, "This is why I told you that no one can come to me unless the Father has enabled him."

Do we believe this? Do we really believe that the next generation can't come to Jesus unless the Father draws and enables them? More pointedly – Do we pray as if we believe it? As I mentioned a few paragraphs ago, my answer is sadly, "No." But I need to. And I am getting better.

PRAY FOR THEM TO LOVE GOD'S WORD.

Our kids are bombarded with messages about who they are (see Principle #5), what they should do, what they should have, and how they should live. As you well know, many of these messages are contrary to what Scripture tells us. How are they going to be able to discern the truth from the lie without a love and understanding of God's Word?

This might sound harsh, but it is not enough for them to believe the Bible is true. Without a love for God's Word they won't read it. They won't engage in conversations about it. They won't talk to their friends about it. And the messages – while true – will get lost in the noisy tidal wave of untrue messages.

We need to pray that the next generation will believe the Bible's veracity – and that they will like it! Pray that they will see the life in the Living Word of God. Pray that they will have engaging, fun, thoughtful conversations about what they read. Pray that their souls will resonate – and even rejoice! – when they hear the truths of Scripture. Pray that the Bible will be so true and so enjoyable that every false message will be so obviously false that they aren't even tempted to believe it.

Pray for the people around them to love God and His Word.

As my kids get older, they are spending an increasing amount of time away from Kari and me. School. Friends. Athletic teams. I know that as the years go by this trend will only increase.

Thankfully, many of their friends love Jesus. And yet, several come from homes of different faith backgrounds – or no faith at all. Kari and I have no desire to completely isolate our kids from any relationships with non-believers. After all, we do want them to "go into all the world and make disciples!" (Mt. 28)

And so we pray. We pray that their friends who already know Jesus would be strengthened in their faith and their own love for God's Word. We pray that their friends who don't know Jesus would come to know Him and the joy and peace that knowing Him brings. We pray that our kids and their friends would "administer God's grace in its various forms" (I Peter 4:10) in their schools, on their teams, with their friends, and throughout our neighborhood.

PRAY FOR PROTECTION.

There is one last element of this principle we need to address before wrapping up this chapter. It is something we don't talk about very frequently in our homes and churches. It has to do with the opposition.

Put clearly: The next generation has an enemy. You have an enemy. Your children have an enemy. The students in your youth group have an enemy. The adorable, innocent kids in your Sunday school classes have an enemy.

I am not trying to over-dramatize this, but all throughout Scripture, God takes the devil pretty seriously. We rarely do. Take a look at these words from the end of Peter's first letter:

Be self-controlled and alert. Your enemy the devil prowls around like a roaring lion looking for someone to devour. (I Peter 5:8)

We typically talk pretty generically about the "impact of culture" or "peer pressure." Don't get me wrong, these are important topics and need to be discussed and addressed. But rarely do we talk about the specific attack our kids and students are under by the one who seeks to deceive them and destroy them. Rarely do we remind our kids that the devil is prowling around. Rarely do we remind them that he is trying to devour them. Yes, it sounds harsh. And it is exactly that harshness that should jolt us into praying fervently for the next generation!

If someone was trying to physically harm one of my kids, it would not take any thought at all to determine whether I would help them. Of course I would instantly fight back! I wouldn't stop fighting off the attacker until my kids were either safe or I was dead.

The last thing the devil wants is for the next generation to be in the habit of regularly entering into and developing a relationship with God through His Word. He knows how dangerous that is! And so he is on the attack. And his attack is on many levels from many angles.

Praying for your children or students is the most effective way to combat this. The stakes are simply too high not to pray

A PRAYER FOR YOUR CHILDREN AND STUDENTS

Lord Jesus, I pray that _____ would fall in love with Your Word. May Your Father draw them to You. (John 6:44) May they hide Your Word in their hearts, that they might not sin against You. (Ps 119:11) May they meditate on it day and night, so that they may be careful to do everything written in it. May they say along with David, "Oh, how I love your law! I meditate on it all day long." (Ps 119:97)

Keith Ferrin is a father, author, speaker,and storyteller. He lives near Seattle with his wife and three kids. Oh...and he really, really likes ice cream. You can connect with him at www.KeithFerrin.com.